A.D. 1882,

28th OCTOBER. Nº 5135

Bicycles and Tricycles.

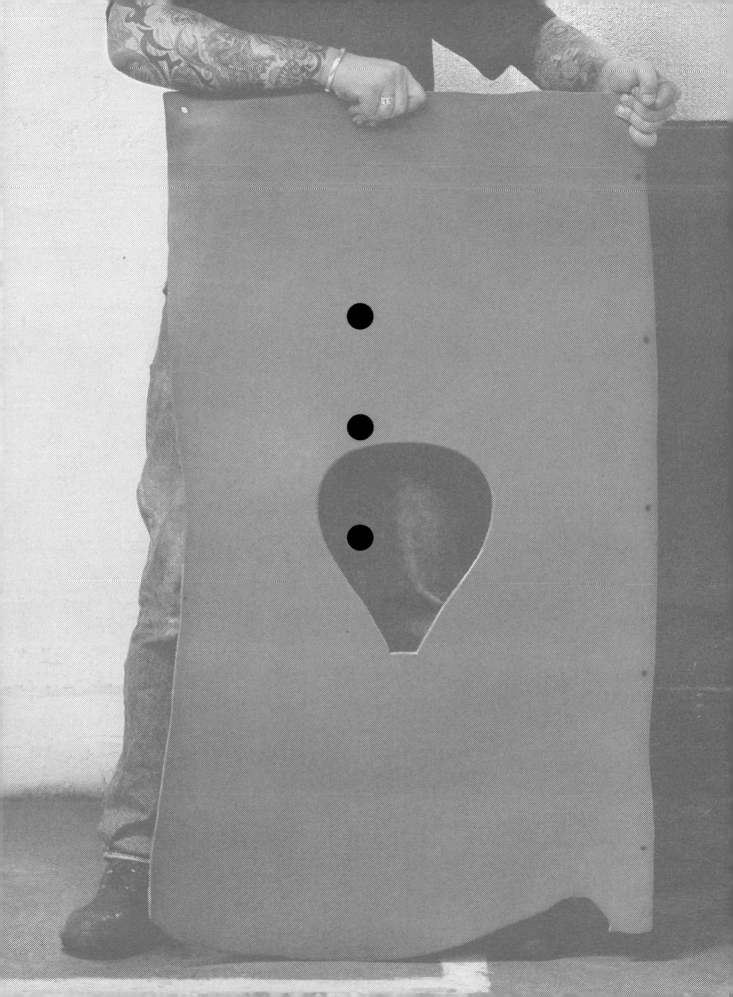

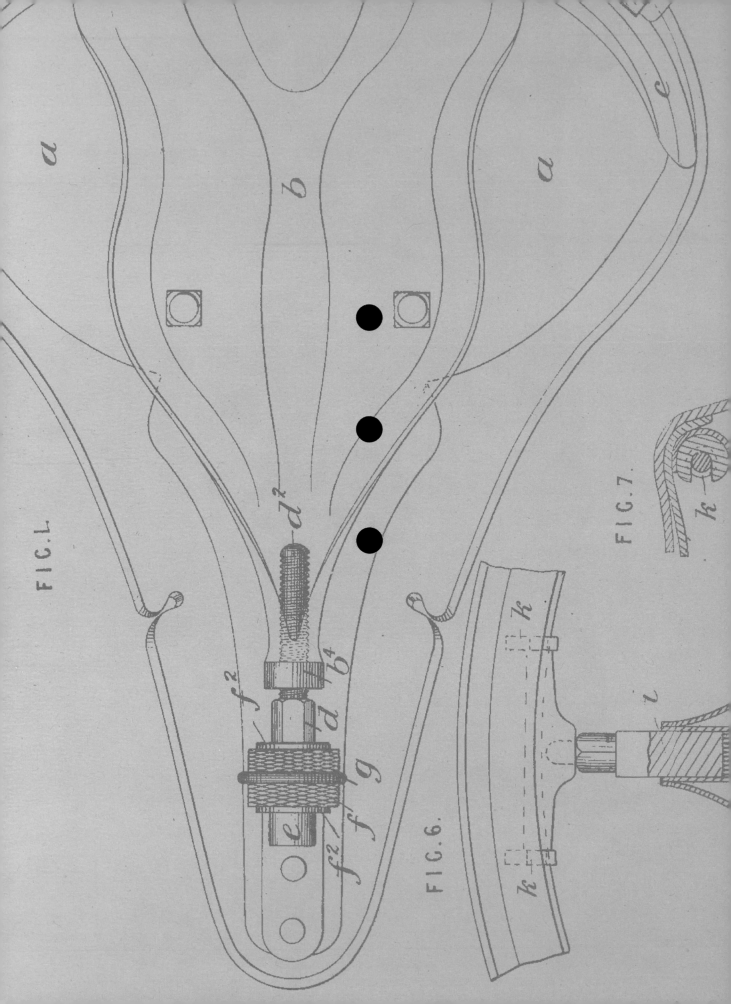

FIC.L.

FIG.6.

FIG.7.

srs. J.B.Brooks & Co.Lt
Gt. Charles Street,
BIRMINGHAM : ENG

Sirs,

You

ing as follows - "SUG
A MORE VALUE TO US IN
INGTON .. BROOKS" - d
sent this cable to Sy
ng Melbourne until t
soon as was expecte

I c
pan and India would
ake the necessary

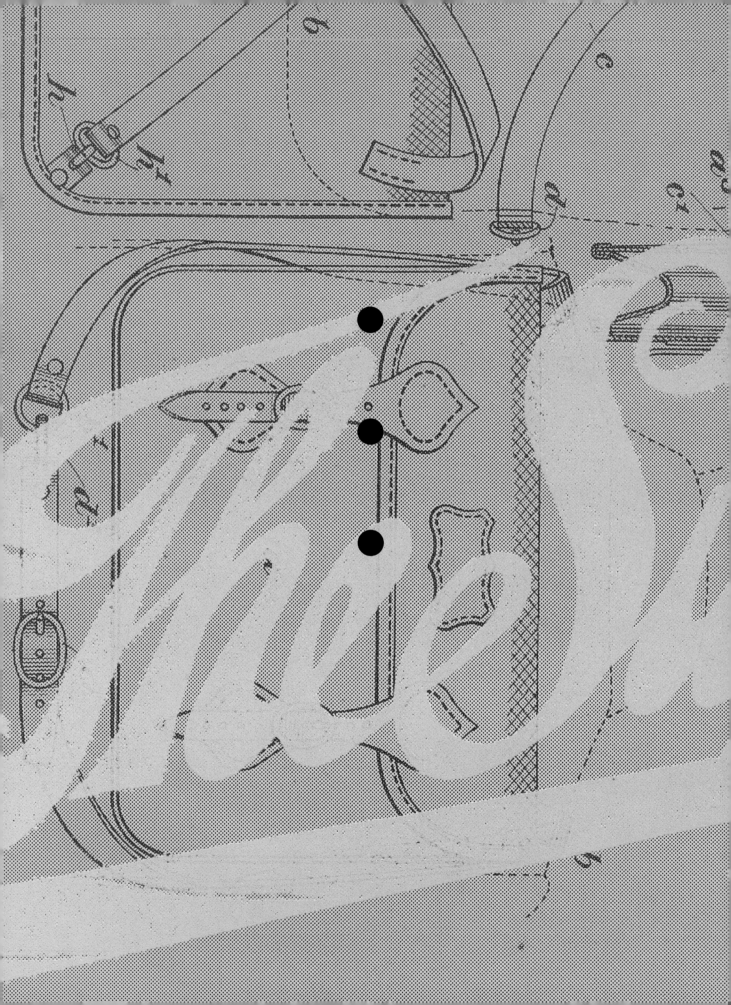

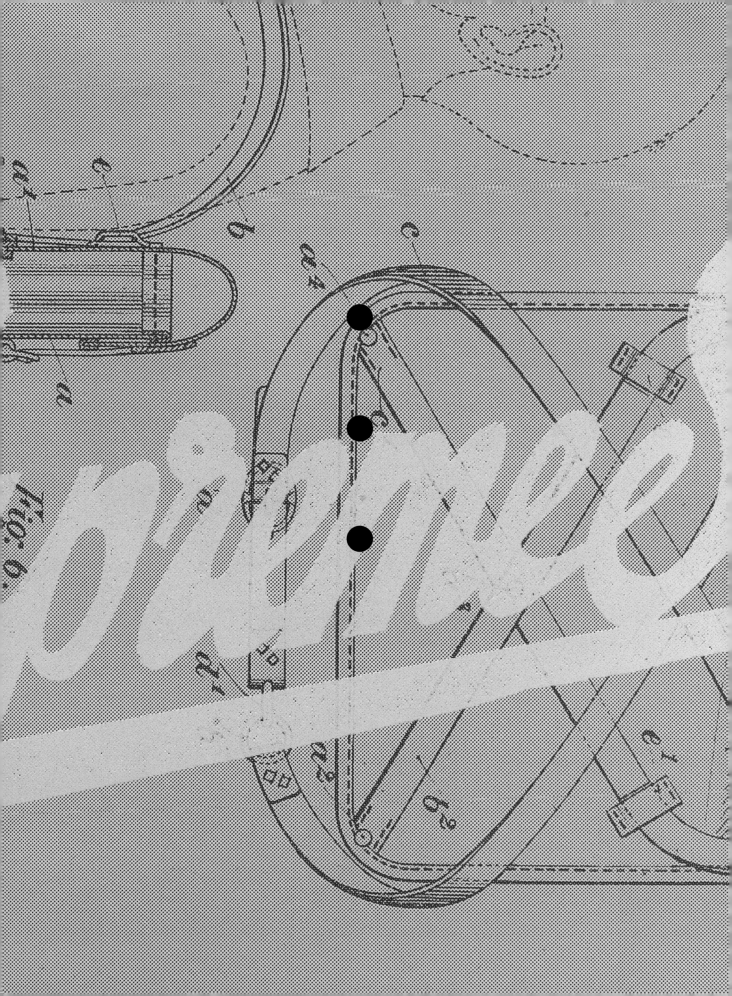

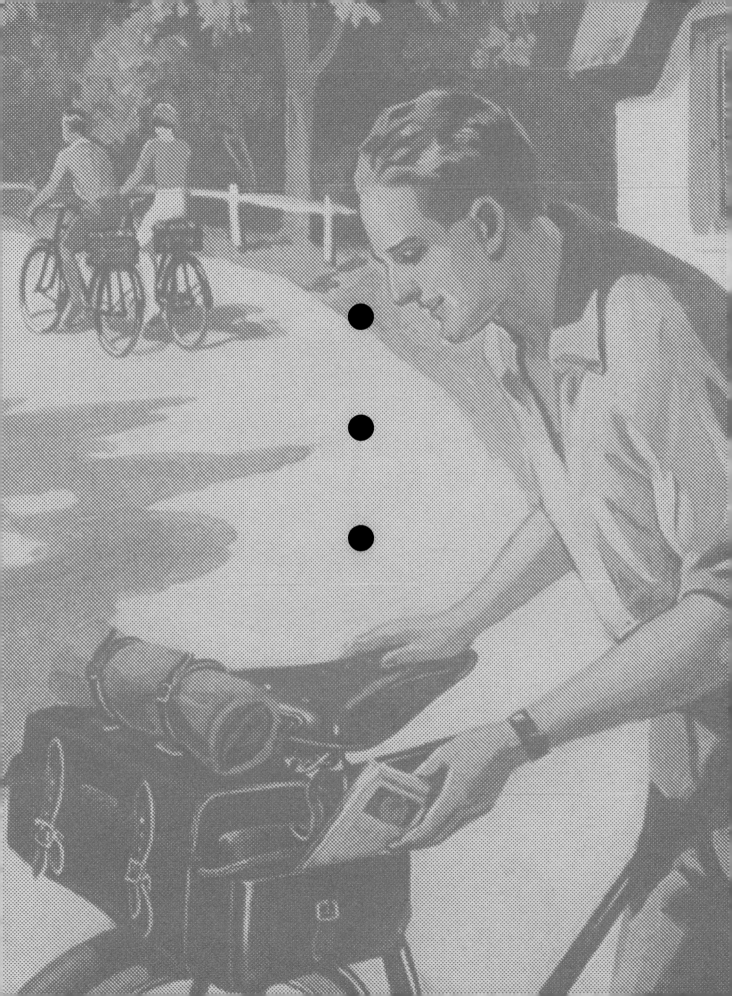

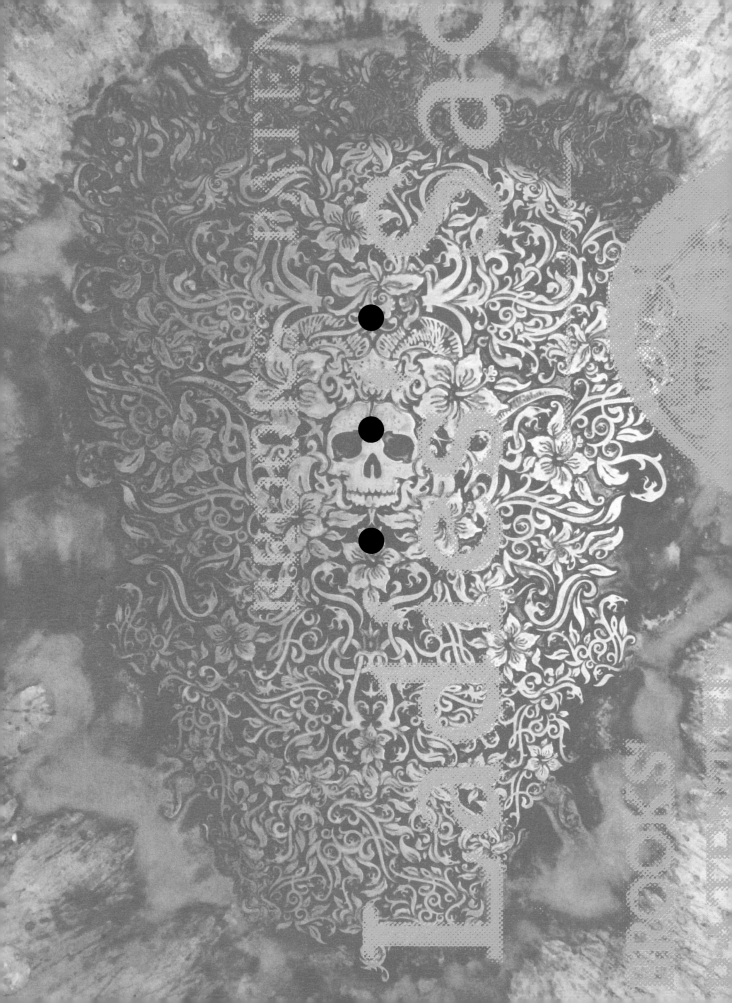

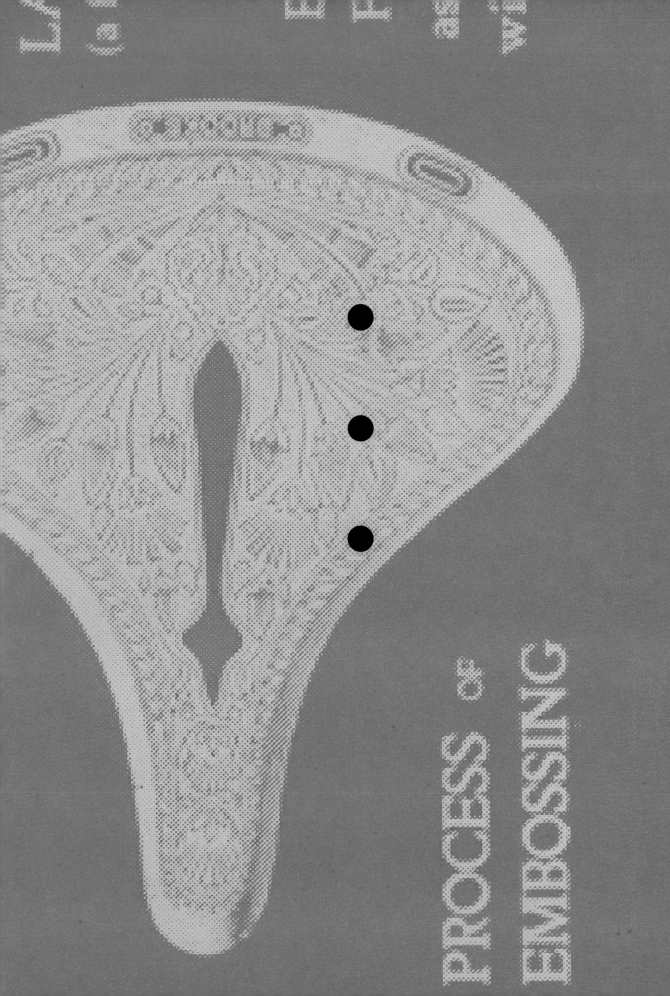

PROCESS OF EMBOSSING

13TH MARCH

ing

The Roa

he sadd

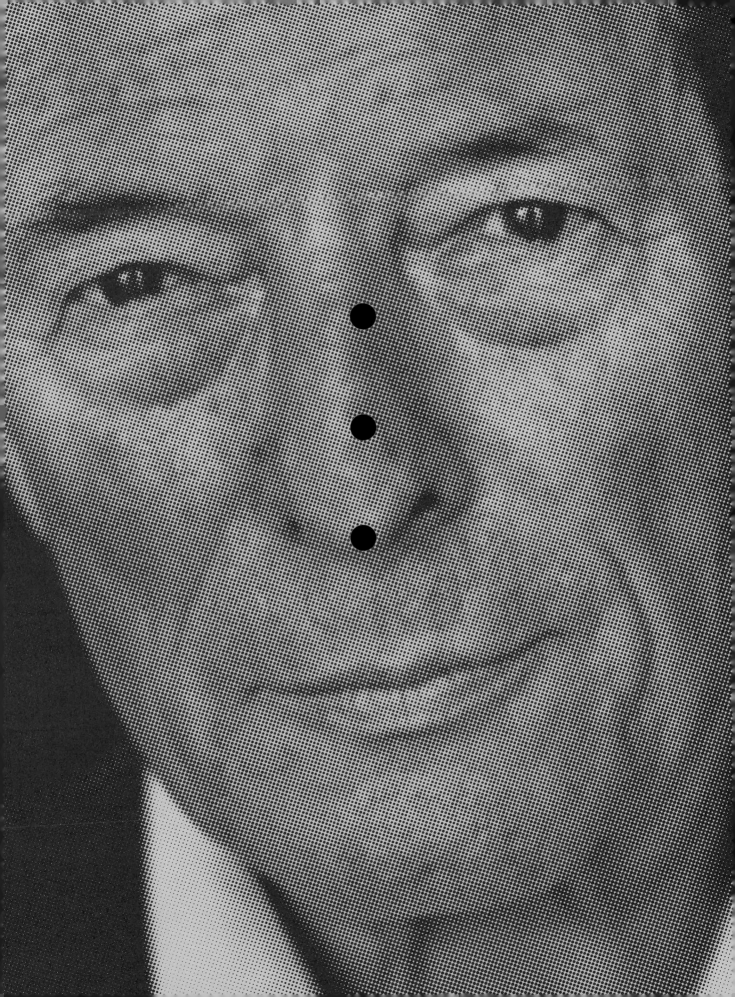

THE
BROOKS
COMPENDIUM
OF CYCLING
CULTURE

RIVETTING STORIES
AND CURIOSITIES
FROM COSMOPOLITAN
GREAT BRITAIN

———————————

A book conceived by

Fabio Fedrigo
Andrea Meneghelli
Michela Raoss

Editor
Guy Andrews

Art Director
Melanie Mues

Thames & Hudson

CONTENTS

PREFACE

This book is not solely about Brooks. It's about the world around Brooks,
the world we get inspired by and the world that we endeavour to inspire with
our products. In the following pages you will not read and see much about
Brooks, only indirectly, and therefore we'd like to take the opportunity
to say something about ourselves now. Hopefully this will give you, our reader,
an idea of where we came from, why we thrived and survived for 150 years
and why we wanted to celebrate our anniversary with this special book, a collection
of stories and curiosities united by a few themes and values we care for.

To begin our story, we wanted to start with a couple of episodes in Brooks's
history: one that we've told before, and one very few people have heard.
Both stories begin with an unexpected event and an epiphany that led to a life
of ingenuity and entrepreneurial success. The first story came to light when,
about ten years ago, we received a letter from Brian Yates, the great-grandson
of John Boultbee Brooks. In this letter he revealed the origins of the Brooks
saddle legend. His father, Henry Bertram Yates, who was the last member
of the family to run the company, from 1941 to 1958, had passed this story
down to him.

In 1865, J.B. Brooks moved from the small town of Hinckley to Birmingham
with £20 in his pocket. In the next year he established himself as a dealer in
general leather goods, under the name of J.B. Brooks & Co. The firm was only
making modest progress until something happened in 1878. Mr Brooks had
been in the habit of riding a horse to and from his business, but this horse died.
Mr Brooks felt he could not afford to buy another, so a friend lent him a bicycle
to make the journey. This introduced J.B. Brooks to cycling, but he found it
so uncomfortable that he vowed he would make something more comfortable
for the rider to sit on. On 28 October 1882, John Boultbee Brooks filed his first
patent, 'Saddles for Bicycles and Tricycles'. The rest, as they say, is history.

The other story begins with a young pharmacist in rural Italy in the mid 1950s.
Dr Riccardo Bigolin had just graduated from university when he applied for
a job at a pharmacy in Rovigo, not far from Venice. When he showed up
at the pharmacy on his first day, another young pharmacist was waiting in front
of the entrance and started talking to Riccardo about his critical situation:
the man had desperately wanted to get Riccardo's job, because he had a wife
and a newborn son. Listening to these words, Riccardo, who was about to
get married himself, decided he could give up the job, return home to Rossano
Veneto and start working at his uncle's felt factory. Soon after, in 1956, he
established Selle Royal, which grew in the following fifty years to become the
world's largest manufacturer of bicycle saddles. This story was told to us by
Barbara Bigolin, Riccardo's oldest daughter, after Riccardo had passed away.
She told us how our parent company was born from an act of generosity.

The paths of our founders never crossed, but those of the two companies
they established did on a few occasions. In 2002 Selle Royal purchased
Brooks from Pashley, who had just saved the company from bankruptcy.
Selle Royal revamped Brooks and gave it renewed impetus to prosper again.

Yet without our founders, J.B. Brooks and Riccardo Bigolin, there would
be no Brooks or this book.

We hope you enjoy every page.

Andrea Meneghclli
Brand Director, Brooks England Ltd

FLOGGING A DEAD HORSE

Illustrations by Joe MacLaren

Our 'dead horse' was John Boultbee Brooks's regular means of transport, a work-a-day steed that in 1878 took him the fifteen miles or so from his home in Finstall Park, Bromsgrove, to his place of work in the City of Birmingham. That morning, when he set out to his stables and found his horse dead, would have been a sad day for Brooks, who had a penchant for riding, bred Shire horses and enjoyed country sports. Nevertheless, he had to get to the factory somehow, so he took off on his borrowed velocipede.

A 'boneshaker' bicycle (as it was known in Britain) wasn't ideal for a long journey – or even a short one for that matter – but he really had to get to work. He had recently acquired the bike, which was state-of-the-art at the time; made from wrought iron with wooden cartwheels shod with iron tyres, it must have weighed a ton; quite literally, a ton. Velocipedes (as they were known in France) were certainly a spreading craze, with their proponents proclaiming, 'I shall have no horse to feed, though I ride a velocipede.' And Brooks was living that dream completely, albeit in unfortunate circumstances.

It wasn't called a 'boneshaker' for nothing. Without pneumatic tyres (yet to be invented) and with a carved wooden saddle, it was an unforgiving cycling experience, to say the least, and Brooks was uncomfortable. (And late for work too, no doubt.) But off he sped on what was possibly one of the first bicycle-to-work commutes in history. It must have been quite an adventure, because in 1878 roads in Britain were few and mostly dreadful cart tracks, making travelling hazardous and uncomfortable. If you were lucky enough to have a horse you could ride above the terrible mire, but this heavy bike must have been an awful chore to propel the few miles Brooks had ahead of him.

Necessity, they say, is the mother of invention, and somewhere along the way Brooks realized that the saddle was the missing link in bicycle comfort. Thus he began to develop the idea for a more comfortable, leather-topped and metal-framed saddle. As Albert Einstein once said about his great discovery, 'I thought of that whilst riding my bicycle.' Brooks was free to think about the problems his journey was throwing at him, and the result was a simple yet ingenious saddle design that was about to make cycling a much more pleasant experience.

Countless commuting trips have started out through a stroke of misfortune. For example, rail strikes in London have created thousands of bike commuters, and when citizens of busy metropolitan areas realize the freedom and convenience a bike allows, they rarely turn back; the idea of being crushed into a train or stuck in a traffic jam on a bus is thereafter unbearable.

People set out on a bike journey, sometimes through choice, sometimes by accident and sometimes because it's the only way to get where they're going. Fast, cheap travel in a busy city is a little like flogging a dead horse; and it's become a joyless part of modern life, precious time spent in limbo between point A and point B. Cycling has changed that for millions of people; the 'iron horse' of the 19th century has become the object for liberation and change for 150 years and into the 21st. Cycle commutes do more than set you free of timetables and traffic jams; these trips allow your mind to wander, to solve and to create. That is true freedom.

So if you reach your bike one morning and realize you have a puncture that will delay your commute, or perhaps force you off the bike altogether, spare a thought for John Boultbee Brooks and his horse. Without this loyal animal's demise, your journey would be a lot more uncomfortable.

BICYCLES, ROMANCE AND
THE WALL OF DEATH
Bella Bathurst

There's an often-quoted theory that it was bicycles that caused the expansion of the European gene pool. A man can walk twenty miles a day, and a horse thirty, but a cyclist can comfortably manage eighty. Instead of having to make do with the small, inbred selection of potential mates from the nearby village, the new cyclist could now go further, faster and for longer – in all senses.

It's a tricky theory to test. By the 1890s, railway travel was ubiquitous. And there was only a brief gap – a generation's span – between the moment in the 1890s when bicycles finally became affordable mass-market objects and the point in the 1920s when automobiles did the same. Besides, without getting too anatomical, how exactly do you quantify cycling's power as an aphrodisiac?

The odd thing about bicycles is that, for as long as they have existed, they have retained their contradictions. Bicycles somehow manage to be comforting, funny and politically radical all at the same time. So when larger numbers of women started riding in the 1890s, opinion was divided between those who regarded it a statement of emancipated modernity, and those who were genuinely appalled to discover that women had legs.

Since women had been riding side-saddle for centuries, it seemed reasonable to think they could do the same with a bicycle. Several manufacturers did experiment with side-saddle frames, but a bicycle is not a horse, and the resulting machines were phenomenally unstable. The obvious alternative – women sitting astride – reduced experts to a froth of euphemisms. Women leaning forward on saddles could only lead to debauchery, debauchery to nymphomania and nymphomania to the ruin of what one French expert called the 'organs of matrimonial necessity'. Civilization's downfall would not be far behind. The Rational Dress Movement joined up cycling, suffragism and the fight against tight lacing through the invention of 'bloomers', loose Turkish-style trousers with a cuff at the ankle, often overlaid with a heavy below-the-knee skirt. When Hoopdriver, the hero of H.G. Wells's *The Wheels of Chance*, sees a woman in full costume cycling past, he is entranced: 'Rational dress didn't look a bit unwomanly … How fine she had looked, flushed with the exertion of riding, breathing a little fast, but elastic and active!'

To anyone in the 21st century, bloomers look ridiculous. But to anyone in the 19th, they must have been a revelation. For women, cycling in normal clothing was almost impossible. Just how cumbersome female dress was at the time was brought home to me when I visited Jackie Reed, a VCC member in Leeds who collects old cycling costume. She allowed me to try on a jacket and skirt from 1905 – the sort of ordinary clothing most women would have worn every day. The skirt was ankle-length and made of a thick, heavy, feltish weave, with a 22-inch waist. The jacket had leg o'mutton sleeves and was designed to be worn with both a corset and a high-collared blouse. With petticoats, the whole outfit would probably have weighed about a stone. With lead in the hems to keep the skirt from blowing, it would have weighed double. And this was the streamlined sports model – the day-wear version came with a train. I struggled to walk without stumbling, and cycling seemed out of the question.

But women did. They cycled because they loved it, and because – like every cyclist since – they recognized that bicycles are the greatest vehicles of escapism ever made, representing escape from drudgery, escape from boredom, escape from the past. Nor did it take women long to discover competitive cycling. At the Royal Aquarium in Westminster, women's bicycle races in the 1890s were relegated to the status of circus acts, competing with bizarre side shows such as 'Chinese edible dogs' and a group called the 'eccentric legmaniacs'. At one women's race in December 1896, the *Pall Mall Gazette* reported that the four women racers appeared, 'in blouses and knickers … (none) was embarrassed by any superabundance of clothing.' In the reporter's opinion, women on bicycles were merely 'an eccentricity in sport'.

So. Did bicycles really expand the gene pool? Are you here because your grandparents were seduced by the twinkle of a diamond frame and the scent of warm tweed? Who knows? Instead, I leave you with the story of the incomparable Zetta Hills, who in 1920 cycled forty-seven miles across the English Channel on her own patent watercycle and went on to cycle a further fifteen miles down the middle of the Thames. To do so, she wore a long skirt, a pair of heeled lace-up shoes, and a broad-brimmed hat. Shortly afterwards she ran off to join Bostock & Wombwell's circus, where she grew strongly attached to a sea lion named Bonzo and became one of the stunt riders on the Wall of Death. An example, I think you'll agree, to us all.

DÍA SIN CARRO
Mark Sutton

In Bogotá, Colombia, the city's population, heading for seven million people, has united on one day a year for the past sixteen years, when an almost unrecognizable calm descends upon its otherwise heaving metropolis. Introduced via referendum at the turn of the millennium by former mayor Enrique Peñalosa to mark Earth Day, their Día sin carro (car-free day) ensures that the Colombian capital is transformed for just over fourteen hours. Around 600,000 private cars are forbidden from the roads from 5 a.m. through to 7.30 p.m. Add to this the city's closure of its streets to cars for the traditional Sunday 'Ciclovía' (in place since the mid 1970s) and the South American state quickly rises on any cyclist's bucket list.

In the past eight years, with a 76% increase in private vehicle registration to contend with, the city has simply ground to a halt. In a tale that is all too familiar for cities battling to cope with rises in pollution, respiratory illnesses see around 600,000 city-dwelling children admitted to hospitals annually for breathing-related issues. Furthermore, for the remaining days of the year, when private vehicle use isn't prohibited, Bogotá's citizens are said to lose an average of twenty-two days a year to sitting in gridlocked traffic.

Fast forward to 2014 and advocacy efforts from Mejor en Bici (Better by Bike) saw the debut of a car-free week; seven days of largely voluntary compliance from citizens who have over time seen the benefits of removing private vehicles from the urban sprawl. Bogotá is by modern standards a friend of the active and home to a great many urban-mobility-obsessed leaders, Peñalosa included. Some 402 kilometres of bike route are extended by a further 63 kilometres for the Earth Day celebration. Residents mark the annual tradition by turning out on bicycles of all shapes and sizes. Bereft even of motorcycles, the roads are a haven for low-cadence chitchat under one's own steam.

Pause for a moment and ponder what your city implementing such a level of traffic reduction might look, sound, or even smell like. For the capital's residents, Earth Day and every Sunday are to be celebrated with both open arms and windows. The world needn't imagine, of course; Car-Free Day is celebrated widely on 22 September in cities around the world. In Europe, for example, Milan, Paris, Amsterdam and Brussels regularly leave the car at home for the odd day. Reykjavík in Iceland has had an annual day off driving since 1996,

and across much of Asia car-free days have been observed for several years, with China and Taiwan having had them regularly since the turn of the 21st century. Better still, every Sunday in Jakarta, Indonesia, is a car-free day. In America, Portland and Washington, D.C. have had car-free days, and many small cities and towns close the roads and keep transport human-powered. But in the UK, only a few towns have had days off driving and although Camden has championed the cause, London is yet to have a 'full' car-free day experience. But wherever in the world you are, the uptake and the enthusiasm is mixed: some commit with gusto, others just quietly close select streets. The aim is to give city-dwellers an idea of what their landscape could be like if the car had never come to fruition on Karl Benz's drawing board 130 years ago. Once a neighbourhood has experienced the liberating peace, the transformation of attitudes is almost universally enthusiastic, venture into a city centre on a car-free day and you'll see pedestrians, cyclists and children roaming as they please. It's only when the cars are not there that you realize the astonishing influence traffic has on our freedom.

Let's not forget, however, that the car set out with genuine intentions to help family mobility and improve our lot. With Ford's launch of the Model T in 1908 – widely considered to be the first accessible car for the masses – the bicycle faced competition for previously tranquil road space (although considerably less of it) from the combustion engine. Famously, today's car industry was born in the minds of cyclists fascinated by taking engineering a step further. In creating the 80-horsepower '999', Henry Ford teamed up with racing cyclist Tom Cooper to build a vehicle driven to success, and ultimately into the hearts of American society following the formation of the Ford Motor Company in 1903. Ford, like Benz before him, was a regular in the saddle.

Despite his role as father of the US motoring business, Ford maintained that the bicycle as a mode of transport was a wise choice as Detroit's industrial restructuring began. Within fifty years the region would begin to see the domination of freeways now so commonly associated with immense numbers of private motor vehicles. Detroit, the American city that is now struggling without its car manufacturing industry, and has become increasingly car-free, but not out of choice and almost in spite of itself.

Might Ford have imagined that the 'car-free day' would ever be required? Or that capital cities around the globe would be going to great lengths to build and legislate the engine out of the modern landscape? In truth, and given his fondness for bicycle transportation, he may well have envisioned

MURATORI'S CAFÉ
Bella Bathurst

Until a few years ago, Muratori's Café stood on London's Farringdon Road opposite the Mount Pleasant sorting office. It's closed down now, but then, it was an old-style kind of caff, a steamed-up greasy spoon with plenty of formica but without the reek of grease. There was wood panelling on the walls and tabloids on the benches, and once in a while someone would emerge from the kitchen with a comment or another pot of tea. The café's place on the corner gave it a grandstand view of the passing traffic, but on a wet February afternoon everyone seemed only too happy to sit tight and offer some lively opinions on the place of cycling within an urban economy.

The following exchange of views is interesting not because it's unexpected but because, for an hour or so, it's salutary to imagine what it must feel like to drive in circles round London's endless frustrations. Most of us cycle because we choose to – we do it for fun, not for work. Which is why it's occasionally worthwhile to consider the view from the other side of the windscreen, and see the city as cabbies do.

Black-cab drivers have always felt like they owned this city. They're part of the place, and – despite Uber's incursions – London would not be the city it is without them. And, since cabbies feel they belong to these streets, one of two things tends to happen. Either they become completely secure in that knowledge and very laid-back about everything, or they become monumentally cross.

the bicycle remaining a prominent fixture of the roads. He would surely have been enthralled by the BBC's cash-cow TV programme *Top Gear* during the episode when the team pitted pedal power against motoring, rail and a speedboat in a race through London that presenter Jeremy Clarkson said 'ruined *Top Gear*'. In what was a nightmare scenario for the programme's petrolhead hosts, the boat came second to Richard Hammond's victorious bicycle in the dash across the UK capital; public transport came third, and the private car lagged some fifteen minutes behind in last place. An average of seven million people tuned in for episodes within that series, cementing the bicycle's seemingly unlikely efficiency in the minds of reluctant motoring fans everywhere. The car may well be king, but the bicycle still proves a compelling heir to the throne.

BB: What do you think of cyclists?

LES (taxi no. 30839): (Pointing at my digital recorder) How much swearing do you want?

BB: That bad?

LES: They are a bit of a nuisance. They're not quick enough, for a start. They creep up the side, they jump lights, they ride across zebra crossings. And we've been told if a bike runs into us, then it's our fault.

BB: So have you ever cut up a cyclist?

LES: No!

UNANIMOUS SHOUTING FROM EVERYONE ROUND THE TABLE: No! No, no, no!

LES: Seriously! Because the last thing I want is a cyclist bashing my cab.

KEITH (taxi no. 30729): Because we know we're on a loser. Even if you do nothing wrong, you're on a loser.

BB: That isn't most cyclists' experience. Most people have been cut up by a cab at some point.

MICKEY (taxi no. 54316): Yeah, OK, but let's say that happens, come up and talk to me, don't bang on the wing mirror and when I get out, cycle off. I've seen a cab and when the guy got out, the cyclist rode round and round tormenting him because he knew any time the guy got near him he could just cycle off.

KEITH: They're so aggressive, aren't they? They bang your bonnet, bang your wing mirror and then they cycle off, they won't stay around to argue. That's what really pisses me off.

BB: Do you think all cyclists are the same?

KEITH: Yeah. You can generalize with cyclists.

BB: So you don't discriminate between couriers and other cyclists?

KEITH: They're all the same. Most of them are the ones travelling to and from work, and they're the ones I can't stand. I've just had so many problems with them over the years. There's been several occasions when they've banged my wing mirrors or bent the aerial off, or hit the cab. I caught one of them once.

LES: You do meet the odd one with the lights on and the yellow stuff all over and the backpacks and everything, and they generally stick to the rules. But the ones who are riding around with next to nothing on, just a bit of Lycra, zooming about delivering stuff, they will take the mickey, no doubt about it. I don't go out of my way to get in their way, but I just find it's hard to avoid them sometimes.

BB: They're just doing a job, same as you.

LES: I understand that, but if they come up the side as they do, if you look at any of our cabs, there'll be little scrape marks along the paintwork. Now, if I go in the garage for that, they'll go, '£50, mate.' I'm not going to get that back off them, never in a million years. And that happens every day.

STEVE (didn't give his driver number): There's a place where all the paramedics go, the guys who deal with all the bad accidents and things, and their entertainment when they're sitting waiting for a call is watching the traffic lights to see how many cyclists stop. They say they actually take a tally. Nine out of ten don't bother.

LES: I don't understand why they've always got to push to the front.

BB: Because if you don't, you're invisible and you're stuck behind some trucker's exhaust.

LES: Yes, but I still don't think, well, I've got to commit suicide, push myself in front of a lorry, just because I'm breathing a bit of crap. I'd sit a few yards back.

KEITH: There should be some sort of registration for them. I know it's difficult and it should be free at first, but they should be registered. Because for every cyclist, that's one less car on the road, and that's great. But you still can't have them all banging and breaking things.

MICKEY: If they knock off your wing mirror, scratch the side of the cab, smash your back light, there's nothing you can do.

There's no comeback. They just ride off. There's no way of recognizing them again. The old cabs used to have a diesel cap on the back. Many times, they just hold onto that and get dragged along by a cab rather than cycle.

LES: A couple of weeks ago, there was a cyclist going the wrong way down Fleet Street. I tooted him and gave him the finger. He came back later and accused me of trying to kill him.

KEITH: You should have done. (General laughter)

LES: I said, 'You're on the wrong side of the road coming towards me, you've got it slightly wrong.' Not in those words, obviously.

PAUL (didn't give his driver number either): You know what it all boils down to? There's no punishment. They don't think the law applies to them.

LES (reflectively): There's a lot of anger, isn't there? A lot of anger coming out of people. See, most cab drivers know we're not going to get anywhere quickly. So we don't drive fast. We know – I've had twenty-nine years' experience of knowing I'm not going to get anywhere. We'll get there eventually, but there's no point in rushing.

BB: But the point is, you can get somewhere quick on a bike.

KEITH: See, that's the trouble. That's their mindset – 'I can get past that, I can go faster, I can get across town.' But they've still got to realize they've got to stop at a red light.

BB: If every cyclist suddenly stopped at every red light, would you start respecting them?

LES: Well, I don't know ...

KEITH: Get 'em off the roads. Cycle lanes, whatever, just get 'em off the roads.

LES: License them!

MICKEY: Round 'em all up and nuke 'em! (General hilarity)

PAUL (looking out of the window at a couple of cyclists coming across the junction towards the café): Hang on, watch that – watch that! He's coming up to the red and ... (the cyclist stops).

Well, he's done it safely, but nine times out of ten they don't. Look! Look! Guy's just gone straight through. He's gone through a red light. Look! He's overtaking!

BB: He's allowed to overtake!

KEITH: Yes, and he's wearing a dirty jumper. And that ain't right. (Gales of laughter) Oh, we don't like cyclists, do we? We hate 'em.

MICKEY: Last summer, June or July it was, there was a naked cycle ride. I was amazed, I was sitting there and there must have been a thousand of them.

BB: So if all cyclists cycled naked, would it make you like them better?

KEITH: Yes. Definitely. They shouldn't be allowed to cycle unless they're naked.

After an hour or so I put away my recorder and get up.

KEITH: There you go, then. Sorry about that. Tell you what, though, we hate bus drivers more. Oh, we really dislike them. So you're not top of the list. And motorbikes. They're third.

In fact, this turns out not to be a comprehensive list. The next time I took a cab, I asked the driver what he thought of other road users. In addition to cyclists, bikers and buses, he added Post Office vans, dustbin lorries and anyone driving a Mercedes. Meanwhile, the view from the other side was equally forthright. At the Westbourne Park Bus Garage, the drivers said they too had a list. Cyclists were the worst. Them, and bloody black cabs.

In the end, all the different transport relationships in London begin to seem a lot like the way things are at the moment with Europe. We might say we hate it and that we want it out of our lives, but when something happens to damage that relationship, we feel bereft. London would be infinitely poorer without its red buses and its black cabs. And, just as fundamentally, without its own cyclists. Live and let live, like we've always done best.

Extract from Bella Bathurst's The Bicycle Book, *published by HarperCollins*

A STREAKING PAST
Guy Andrews

Unless you listened to BBC Radio 4's morning news reports over the years between 2004 and 2010 then you've probably never heard of Stephen Gough. Otherwise known as the 'Naked Rambler', or by his self-given moniker the 'Prisoner of Conscience', Gough was in the media a lot at the time, for trying to walk the length of the UK from Land's End to John o' Groats with a rucksack and wearing nothing but a pair of walking boots. While his naked quest initially appeared typically British and eccentric, it became, for a brief time, the topic of mildly embarrassed debate at the breakfast tables of many households across the UK. The more you learn about the case the more you start to question the point of it all.

Now, I'm no naturist, but I reached the point where I just wanted the Naked Rambler to make the distance, mostly because he was having such a torrid time of it with the authorities. He'd been arrested twenty-odd times the first time he arrived in Scotland, and eventually served a variety of prison sentences totalling up to six years. Many said he was wasting public money and police time, and perhaps they had a point, but to most it just seemed extreme to want to walk across the UK naked in the first place, what with the weather as it is. Nevertheless he eventually made it, and call it what you will – a protest, a gesture of freedom or just a publicity stunt – but Stephen Gough's naked crusade sparked much debate. He gained some support and a small following, albeit by those sympathetic to the underdog and those happy with the idea of 'breaking the mould'.

If you can excuse the pun, the Naked Rambler exposed a tendency in the British psyche to be alarmed and at the same time titillated by the idea of naturism. It's something that the usually reserved British mentality endlessly struggles with. The law isn't particularly draconian towards nudity (and freedom of speech has always been a cornerstone of protest and debate in the UK) and public opinion on stripping off is generally sympathetic to the right to dress (or undress) as you wish and to express yourself, as long as you don't cause too much of a fuss.

Strangely, 'baring all' is something that has always been in the mind of British cyclists. In the 1970s one particular poster became hugely popular to have hanging on your wall, albeit surreptitiously, in the back of a bike shop workshop or washroom. It was that of a still from the video of rock band Queen's 1978 hit single *Bicycle Race*. The late, great British cycling broadcaster and journalist David Duffield was working as a marketing manager for Halfords at the time and supplied the sixty-five bikes for what, unbeknown to him, could be described as the world's first naked mass bike ride.

One late summer's evening, around the time police were pointlessly and somewhat hilariously chasing the Naked Rambler over the Pennines, I was driving through some horrendous central London traffic in an estate car full to the brim with bikes. There were four on the roof rack and five inside with wheels sat around me creating an uncomfortable nest of spokes, axles and rubber. The car resembled a crammed bike shed on wheels, though a stationary one – it was gridlock. Up ahead there were frustrated cabbies chatting with one another through open windows and resigned commuters who had turned their engines off. The buses emptied as the passengers took to the pavement. Those left to sit it out 'were the traffic', and it was static. After many minutes a few cyclists appeared and started to pick their way through the gaps between the lines of cars, taxis and buses. A while longer and the few became a stream, in and around the stranded commuters who all stared agog: the hundreds of noisy demonstrators were made all the more astonishing by virtue of the fact that each and every one was naked.

After a few minutes readjusting to this new scene, I sat there surrounded by naked cyclists. A cyclist myself, sitting fully clothed in a marooned car full of bikes, I felt slightly embarrassed, not because I'm prudish, but because the contrasts were overwhelming, added to the fact I had literally nowhere to go. A couple of the bare-arsed bikers even shouted at me to 'drop them and get on one of those nice shiny bikes'. Eventually the naked procession passed by, the cabbies raised their eyes to the skies and we all pulled away to limp through the remains of the day's rush hour. It made me think, though, about two things: what on earth were they doing, and why was one of the butt-naked riders wearing nothing but a matching pair of arm- and leg-warmers?

Confused, I asked a few fellow London cyclists what they knew. It transpired that the World Naked Bike Ride was becoming a phenomenon in many cities across the USA and Europe, especially those challenged by poor safety conditions for cyclists. Various incarnations of riding naked had been around for a while, but the World Naked Bike Ride was 'officially' inaugurated in 2003 by Conrad Schmidt and a group of like-minded artists in British Columbia, Canada to 'deliver a vision of a cleaner, safer, body-positive world'. It was, perhaps, an idealist's approach to protest naked, but their intention was to show the vulnerability of cyclists and to emphasize the human aspect of city cyclists' problems as being central to their message, although it also set out to highlight more generally the state of the world oil industry, globalization and waste. Nudity wasn't compulsory, but participating riders were encouraged to 'bare as you dare'.

Protesting about road conditions in London was nothing new. Critical Mass, a monthly protest ride, had been going on

for many years; it was fairly radical and polarized opinions. Some endorsed the direct-action approach, others thought it unnecessary and too confrontational. I joined it once and found the experience a little perplexing, although their motto, 'we are not stopping traffic, we are traffic', is as plain a truism as you can get on the traffic issue. Unfortunately not everyone saw it that way – many other road users reacted angrily, and sometimes violently, towards the protesting riders. TV anchors, radio talk-show hosts and newspaper columnists endlessly tutted, disapproved, wrote the demonstrations off as just a bit of a nuisance and went on simply to criticize cyclists for jumping red lights and riding on the pavements. It all somehow seemed to be missing the point. And, as the saying goes, lose your temper and you lose the debate, meaning that neither side of the argument has achieved very much at all. The British comedian and avid cyclist Alexei Sayle summed up my thoughts on the resulting paradox, that of direct action and flouting the law, when he said, 'if you start to behave like car drivers you become just the same as them…'. And when it comes to jumping red lights and 'over-asserting' oneself, most regular cyclists know it's better to obey the laws of the road.

So where did it all go wrong?

It's complicated, but the crux of city traffic issues has threads going all the way back to the oil crisis of 1973. This proved a turning point for many countries, and while the UK ground to a halt, the more forward-thinking European cities, such as Amsterdam and Copenhagen, decided to start to change the way that traffic moved in their urban areas. These changes had been coming for a while; at first it wasn't all about the bike or the oil, it was a lot more serious than that. In 1971, the deaths of children on Dutch city streets

had reached an annual count of around 400, so families decided to get together and demand change. As a result, the city councils legislated heavily to calm car driving completely, and made space for cyclists. They drastically reduced speed limits and generally shunned motorized transport in favour of walking and cycling. The result was less car ownership, close to 100% bike ownership and a healthier, happier and safer environment for their citizens.

Those cities that experience near car-free environments are simply better places to be; that's a fact. So if you ride a bike in any city in the world and feel the need to change the conditions you're cycling in, then at least appreciate that the demonstrators are trying to achieve that end. It's about time the political will changed on a global scale now there has been a shift in opinion since the early days of protest; regular demonstrations by disgruntled cyclists are gaining more popular support. The London-based pressure group Stop Killing Cyclists and the regular Die-Ins in cities across the world (where riders simply block off streets and squares and lie on the ground) have started to receive more favourable media coverage, and in many ways are emulating the positive and brass-tacks stories of the unfortunate citizens of Amsterdam nearly fifty years ago.

Around the globe the World Naked Bike Ride remains a well-behaved, non-violent and, actually, fun protest, a thought-provoking demonstration that has changed the way many people view the issues facing cyclists. I would never suggest that someone simply strip off and do a Stephen Gough by riding down their local high street starkers, but if you are a regular cyclist with an eye on the future, you owe it to those who have gone before to do your bit. Perhaps, then, we should all get naked every once in a while?

[NOT] JUST HERE FOR THE BEER
Guy Andrews, Matt Brammeier
and Tom Southam

In Belgium the bicycle is king. In Flanders, and specifically west Flanders, bicycle racing isn't just a part of the culture, it *is* the culture. Everyone knows about cycling, and of this country's six million people, at least a third turn out on Easter weekend to watch their home race: the Tour of Flanders. And if cycling is their entertainment, then beer is undoubtedly their refreshment. Sint-Eloois-Winkel is a small town, and like most Belgian towns it brews a fine beer, called Steene Molen. The brewery decided that for their national race in 2015 they would organize a competition within the race. The first rider across a line in the town would win their body weight in beer, which is where Matt Brammeier, a professional bike racer for Team Dimension Data, picks up the story:

> I was sitting on the team bus before the race and flicking through Twitter and I saw [ex-pro rider] Dan Lloyd had tweeted something about this beer prize, so I drew a beer mug on a sticker to put next to the distance references already marked on my handlebar stem – it was a bit of a joke at first. My goal for the day was to get in the early breakaway anyway, which I did. When we got to Sint-Eloois-Winkel, though, I had no idea where the line for the sprint was; I just knew I needed to be near the front going through the town, so I just went for it. And won.

> It was around seventy bottles of beer, so I had to give most of it away. The team had a pretty bad race, so they were pretty happy that I managed to get something out of it, even if we did give most of it to the mechanics. But I made it into the break, and it got a fair bit of publicity.

There, in a nutshell, is the purpose of professional bike racing: PR. It's not all about winning; it's just as much about getting the jersey on the TV and in the papers. Such is the character of Matt Brammeier, all in to help the team but with an eye on the prize and a bit of fun. Fast forward a couple of seasons and Matt got caught up in some terrible crashes. Recuperating gave him time to think, and one thing was bugging him. At the start of any racing season a professional bike rider will receive a delivery of kit, along with three or four bikes and enough helmets, pairs of sunglasses and shoes to kit out a national team – he thought it seemed excessive, wasteful even. You can't use it all, so what to do with it?

Contrast that, then, with riders racing in the Tour of Rwanda. Tom Southam was once a professional bike racer, turned his skills to writing upon retirement and nowadays works as a team manager, but it was a piece he wrote about a visit to that race that opened many professional riders' eyes to the conditions their African counterparts had to put up with, as Tom recalls:

> Early on at the Tour of Rwanda, I met an Ethiopian rider who hit a pothole and crashed during one of the opening stages, I think he had cracked the frame, or some such. And he was absolutely gutted. When I tried to give him the old, 'oh well don't worry, there are more races', he insisted that the problem wasn't missing the race, it was his broken bike. There were no bike shops at all in Ethiopia. The riders had to get together and buy a container full of old frames and equipment from Gazelle in Holland. There were no plans to order more equipment for at least a year, which meant that the guy simply couldn't ride, so that was it. There was no other option for him; he would have to effectively give up cycling for twelve months, find a job, and try to get enough money together to buy a frame and try again. The timeline was ludicrous, and it struck me that things were stretched so thin, that one small crash in a race could end it all for any one of these guys.

> The equipment that was used in the Tour of Rwanda was extraordinary, in a bad way. I think that the team from Tanzania were the worst off. One of them got his chain caught between the frame and the cassette on the first stage; we came across him desperately trying to fix it in the middle of the road. I ended up getting out of the 4x4 and fixing it for him, and the bike was a wreck. You honestly wouldn't steal it if it was left leaning up against the wall outside the pub over a Saturday night, and this was the first stage – not the last one.

> The money doesn't just go on equipment for bikes though, it's the whole thing. We had to give all of the food we had on us to one of the Ethiopian riders on stage three. The team had started the race with no food at all. Nothing. It was a 150-kilometre stage that went straight uphill; the Ethiopians had smashed the race to bits out of the blocks, then one by one they just blew up. We worked out later that they didn't know to take any food with them. It blew my mind that they were even competing without eating anything during the stage at all. In Europe there are people in teams whose whole job it is to make sure that the guys have the right food at the right time, as well as the trainers and so on, to educate them as to what to eat and when. In Africa people just helped, in whatever way they could.

After joining MTN–Qhubeka (now Dimension Data) at the beginning of 2015, Matt Brammeier's kit frustration took a turn towards a solution when he met up with new team-mate Adrien Niyonshuti. Adrien was caught up in the Rwandan genocide in 1994, when six of his brothers were murdered. His story is compelling to say the least – from impoverished and tragic circumstances, to being recognized as a considerable talent, to eventually winning the Tour of Rwanda, joining a professional team and ending up rooming with Matt, who picks up the story again:

He told me where he came from and where he got to being the first Rwandan cyclist to race in the European professional peloton – he's the biggest inspiration imaginable. After that, whenever I got my race programme through, if I saw Aidy's name on the list it always made me smile. But it was talking to Adrien and him telling me what kit and conditions they were racing in – they had no helmets or cycling shoes and rode three-speed bikes – listening to Adrien's stories made me think, and this idea smacked me right in the face.

I never used to like the waste of it all, the fact that we had way more kit than we needed. So I used to send it all back to my old cycling club, which was cool, getting this stuff to kids like me who wanted a bit of extra kit to get them going. Cool, I thought, but what would be even cooler would be to get this stuff to people who didn't just want it, but really needed it.

So the idea was simple: to take any cycling gear that's in a presentable and useable condition, preferably small sizes for kids, and send it out to the Adrien Niyonshuti Cycling Academy in Rwanda. We've already sent around 2,000 pieces of clothing on a big pallet, that's something like half a ton of clothing that's already gone to Rwanda and some to South Africa. We've sent a lot of stuff in suitcases too, with riders and friends travelling back and forth to South Africa. We stuff bike bags with some too, sometimes. It's not just clothing, it's shoes, helmets, sunglasses. In some African countries it's pretty complicated just getting the stuff through customs; we want to send some kit to other countries like Kenya and Eritrea, but it's hard to even get it into those countries. Some guy once tried to get 5,000 pairs of shoes into Africa to give away and they wanted $5 a pair for the customs clearance; it just isn't worthwhile, it ends up costing too much.

So far, most of the stuff has come from team-mates and friends, it's been a great response. I got a message from Italian professional rider Matteo Trentin, who said that his mother had been through his old wardrobe and filled five bin bags with old clothing and he was asking me, how can he get it to me? And companies have been good too, sending old stock and the like – it's been an overwhelming response. We can't really make things much bigger just yet: when you start thinking it would be cool to send bikes, then you're talking containers and it just becomes too costly, and anyway there's already a charity called Re-Cycle doing a scheme through Halfords' shops that makes sure old bikes get sent on to people who need them.

After ten years, just getting up and racing a bike gets a bit boring, so it's been refreshing to do something else. The team also went to South Africa to see what the Qhubeka charity do down there, and it really impressed me – Qhubeka take the principle a step further: bicycles mean you get to school faster, you're able to work and to help others. In a continent where 250 million people have no access to transport at all, this reason alone is their motivation. Now I'm just really thankful that the team have given me the time and support to do the kit appeal – it certainly feels good to be giving something back to help others while I'm still racing.

I know it sounds cliché to say that 'bicycles change lives', but I really believe they do; they certainly changed mine for the better.

————————

There are plenty of opportunities to help those who help people change their lives with bikes. The next time you go to the bike shop, maybe stop and think about what you don't need and what you can pass on, because somebody, somewhere, will make good use of it.

Adrien Niyonshuti's Cycling Academy in Rwanda – ancycling.org
Team Dimension Data–Qhubeka – bicycleschangelives.org
Mobilizing people through the power of bicycles – worldbicyclerelief.org
Secondhand bikes to Africa – re-cycle.org
Africa Kit Appeal (Matt's charity) – africakitappeal.com

GREAT BRITISH
INGENUITY

Guy Kesteven
Photographs by Antony Cairns

GREAT BRITISH INGENUITY

An Englishman's home is his castle, but the workshop is where he is king

It'd be fair to say that most countries aren't quite sure what to make of the British. They love our music, they laugh at our TV shows – and laugh even harder at our food. For the most part, though, we're irritatingly independent, deliberately awkward and awash with a stubborn self-righteousness, sensing, somehow, that we always know best.

A remarkable mindset, considering our once mighty empire is now essentially reduced to a couple of diligently defended but diminutive rocky lumps populated by barbary apes and sheep. But while the world might not know exactly what to make of us, they do know that we are brilliant at making stuff they'd probably never have thought of. So why do we have such a reputation for innovation, and why (and how) have we created so many world-changing inventions?

You don't have to shake the tree of invention history that hard to realize it's rarely just a case of waiting for an apple to drop and recognizing the gravity of the situation. OK, so that's not the best example, but even when Isaac Newton stopped dodging fruit long enough to build the first reflecting telescope it took a century for mirror technology to catch up.

Some of the most significant inventions ever were almost stopped in their tracks by the very colleagues of inventors. Tommy Flowers's war- and world-changing development of the world's first electronic programmable computer – the code-breaking Colossus – was nearly halted after an accusation that it was just 'squandering good valves' from other Bletchley Park inventors. Although Frank Whittle had a working prototype of his turbojet engine by April 1937, lack of interest from the UK government meant British pilots were still fighting the first German jets from behind propellers in 1944. Cyclists will weep onto their composite top tubes when they hear that the chance to exploit the Ministry of Defence's pioneering work with carbon fibre structures was thrown away when the government sold off the nationalized Rolls-Royce carbon fibre plant and other UK licensed producers concentrated on low-cost, not high-quality, developments. Meanwhile, the Japanese government pumped big money into its own carbon constructors, and that's why bike shops are full of bikes built from Toray and Mitsubishi – not Courtaulds or Rolls-Royce – fibres.

Even those directly involved in some of the greatest moments of invention weren't always impressed by the experience. When prolific Yorkshire inventor George Cayley flew one of his servants across the dale in front of his house in 1804 in his revolutionary glider, the first ever fixed-wing pilot reportedly resigned as soon as he landed. Churlish indeed considering Cayley had created the first tension- rather than compression-spoked wheels to absorb the shock of landing. That makes him the only person who can rightfully claim to have re-invented the wheel, and it paved the way for his 'Universal Railway' wagons, which used a primitive pioneering form of tank-style caterpillar track. He also invented a self-righting lifeboat that would have solved the problems faced by another inventor saddled with an unappreciative test team: the local boatmen

INCANDESCENT LIGHT BULB

Humphry Davy, 1802

It's one of the great ironies of the history of invention that the original 'light bulb moment' was actually one of the more tortuous development processes on record. There was almost a century between the first spark of an idea and the production of an incandescent bulb that lasted long enough to be worth buying. Contrary to pub quiz folklore it wasn't Thomas Edison who 'invented' the light bulb either. Cornish inventor Humphry Davy first created light by passing an electrical current through a carbon filament. However, his subsequent fascination with the intoxicating effects of nitrous oxide (laughing gas), rather than incandescence, literally put Davy off the scent – and frequently on his back.

Seventy years later, Thomas Edison was so bored working through thousands of different filament, inert gas and vacuum combinations that he invented the phonograph so that he had something to listen to. But his diligence eventually extended bulb lifespans from 40 hours to 1,500, making Edison a household name. Electrifying stuff.

employed by George Manby to test his 'unsinkable ship', already annoyed at the shipwreck booty they were losing as ships were saved by his rescue-rope firing 'Manby Mortars', deliberately overturned his boat – which stayed afloat even when filled with water – out of spite. Suspicions that Manby's people skills may not have been as natural as his inventing flair are borne out by the fact that his revolutionary harpoon design was deliberately sabotaged by the very whalers he'd sailed all the way to Greenland to show it to. It's a credit to his essential love of a seemingly ungrateful human race that he still went on to develop the first self-contained, portable, pressurized fire extinguisher, was the first to advocate for a national fire brigade and was instrumental in the creation of the Royal National Lifeboat Institution.

In other cases the true importance of inventions wasn't even fully grasped by the creators themselves. Even something as brilliant as the electric light bulb didn't manage to hold the interest of its inventors as well as it does moths. Cornishman Humphry Davy first created light by passing electricity through a carbon filament in 1802, but spent so much time stoned while developing laughing gas that his most memorable contribution to lighting was a primitive miner's lamp: a candle in a mesh cage. That meant it was Joseph Swan who was left to exploit Davy's discovery by putting the carbon filament in a partial vacuum to extend burn times. Except he didn't. While his incandescent glory glowed briefly, in 1860 the quality of electrical supply and vacuum available genuinely sucked and by the time he picked up the (carbonized) thread again in 1878, Edison was already well ahead in terms of developing sustainable electric lighting. Swan did at least get a nod from fellow English inventors Bulpitt & Sons Ltd when they started the Swan brand, just down the road from Brooks in Birmingham. As one of the first Swan products was an electric kettle they can rightly claim to have made a massive contribution to UK inventors everywhere, by providing that most essential problem-solving ingredient: a good cup of tea.

While disinterest and distraction might have hobbled some inventors, others met outright hostility when their ideas came to light. John Kay doubled the speed of looms overnight in 1738 when he introduced his revolutionary fly-shuttle mechanism. He also had to escape from Lancashire to Leeds double-quick to escape murderous weavers who thought their jobs were under threat from the new invention. The doubled appetite of the looms meant spinning technology was crying out for a similar mechanized revolution, but because of the violent resistance to change, James Hargreaves kept his eight-spindle

TOOTHBRUSH
WILLIAM ADDIS, 1770

Toothbrushes are the number one material for carving makeshift weapons (or shivs) in prison, and ironically that's where they were first made. Whether it was his breath or the state of his teeth that caused the riot William Addis was accused of starting in 1770 isn't recorded. However, by the time he was released from prison for the offence, he had perfected a method for threading bristles through the head of bone handles to create the ultimate tooth cleaner. Just short of 250 years later the Wisdom company he founded manufactures over 70,000,000 toothbrushes a year in the UK. That idea scrubbed up well then.

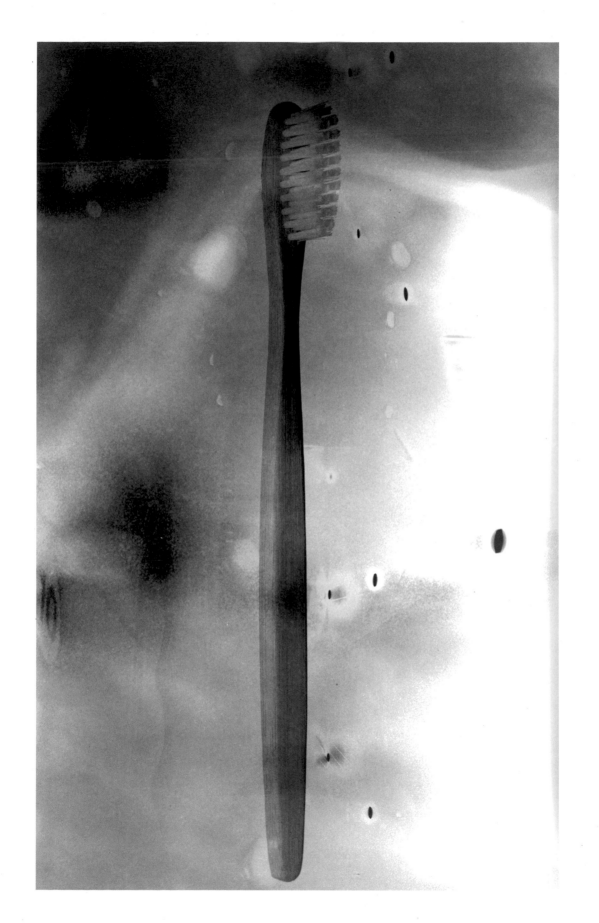

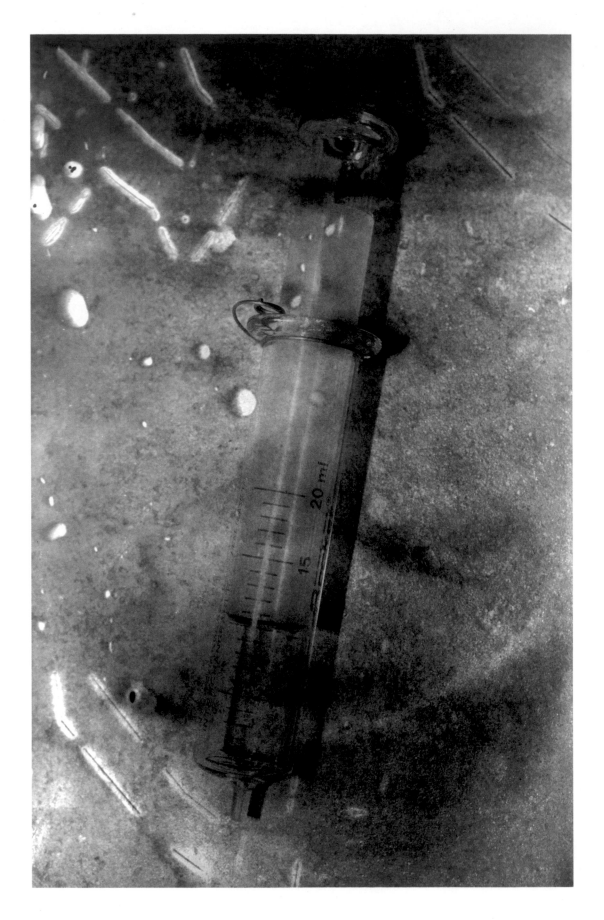

GREAT BRITISH INGENUITY

HYPODERMIC SYRINGE

Dr Alexander Wood, 1851

Occasionally something so radical comes along that there isn't even a word to describe it. Irish surgeon Dr Francis Rynd pioneered injection through the skin in 1844, but it was Scotsman Dr Alexander Wood who made the first glass syringes for accurate dosage in 1851. It was only in 1858 that London-based surgeon Dr Charles Hunter invented the phrase 'hypodermic' and noticed that anaesthetics still worked if injected away from the site of the injury. Hunter's work obviously got under Wood's skin in other ways, though, and the two spent several years needling each other in the law courts. A prickly business indeed.

BROOKS LEATHER SADDLE

John Boultbee Brooks, 1878

Some inventions evolve over time but eventually come full circle as innovation icons, and that's true of the Brooks B17 saddle (photographed overleaf). It only made its debut in the Brooks range a decade after John Boultbee Brooks's cycle commuting misery inspired him to create his first tension-framed leather saddle. Introduced as a relatively broad 8½ in. all-rounder, it slimmed to 6½ in. width as the Champion before the first 6-in. Narrow fleetingly appeared in 1910, becoming a range regular in the 1920s. Thinner, split-topped, chromed, stainless and cutaway versions all followed and the B17 Competition of 1959 became the first saddle to use a dedicated Campagnolo seat pin. A century after the original appeared, it is the Narrow and the laced-and-slotted Narrow Imperial that have endured in the Brooks range as the few items on the modern road bike that would still be instantly recognizable to a rider from a hundred years ago. Truly iconic.

Spinning Jenny machines secretly hidden for four years. The increasingly irate spinners of Blackburn were determined to find out how Hargreaves was creating such large amounts of cheap yarn though and broke into his workshop in 1768, smashing the Jennies while Hargreaves fled to Nottingham.

Sometimes it was exactly the opposition that inventors met that made them come up with even bigger, better solutions. At the same time as Hargreaves was on the run, John Kay was working in secret with another Lancashire entrepreneur, Richard Arkwright, to produce water-powered spinning machines. These were so successful that Arkwright soon built the first water-powered cotton mill at Cromford, in Derbyshire, to house as many of them as possible. More machines needed better-organized workers to man them, and with the mill came the first employment contracts, time rather than daylight-measured shifts and even a village to house the workers' families. No surprise then that Arkwright was soon hailed as the father of the Industrial Revolution.

An environment of progression always creates extra momentum for evolution, and while Arkwright's factory ideas undoubtedly formed part of the essential fabric of the Industrial Revolution it was other industrious revolutionaries who literally got it up to steam. Preacher Thomas Newcomen swapped religious hot air for hot water to create the first useful steam-powered atmospheric pumping engine in 1712. James Watt's engine of 1775 reversed the piston-sucking condensation design of Newcomen and used the more efficient and powerful pressure of expanding steam to drive rotary shafts. Now machines that had previously relied on water power could be driven by steam engines, so mills and factories could be built wherever their owners wanted. More powerful double opposing pistons and compound engines followed and soon Watt's engines were not only driving the Industrial Revolution but also adding his name and his phrase, 'horse power', to the power-measuring lexicon.

They came just in time for a world that was rapidly seeing the mechanical replacing the biological, meteorological and geographical on land and sea. Cornishman Richard Trevithick mounted a pumping engine on wheels to create his 'Puffing Devil' in 1801, while Richard Wright fitted a steam engine to a French fishing boat to create the first sea-going steamboat, aptly named 'Experiment', ten years later. By 1830 George Stephenson had literally put passenger-carrying railways on the map with the Liverpool and Manchester Railway. Legendary engineer Isambard Kingdom Brunel took passenger travel to a whole new level. By combining his Great Western Railway with a series of ocean-going steamships he created the first regular, scheduled passenger service from London to America. Ironically, while Brunel's final ship, SS *Great Eastern*, never managed the non-stop trips to India it was designed for, it did help to lay the first reliable transatlantic telegraph cable in 1866, starting another exponential explosion in global communication.

GREAT BRITISH INGENUITY

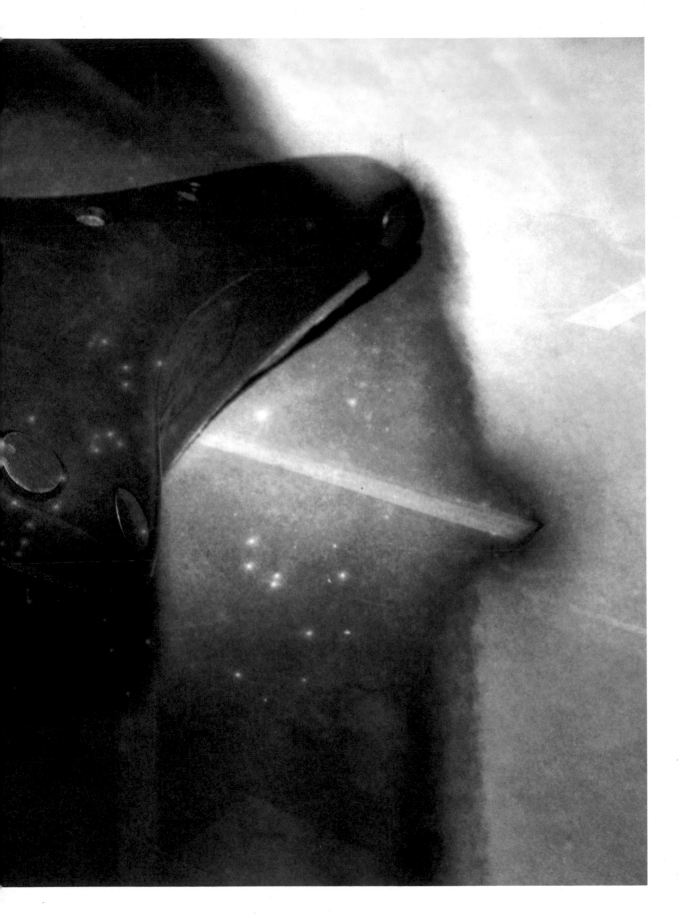

BUSH ROLLER CHAIN
Hans Renold, 1880

While some inventors never receive recognition or reward for their products, others are astute enough to make the most of it. Hans Renold had only bought his small textile chain company a year before inventing the metal bush roller chain in 1880. Its combination of efficiency and durability was perfect for the new generation of 'safety' bicycles that were being built. His business expanded rapidly, and Renold PLC is still one of the leading chain and transmission manufacturers today. It wasn't just Hans who profited either, as he was renowned for excellent treatment of his workers and even left his house to be used by the company's 'social union' after his death.

PNEUMATIC TYRE
Robert Thomson, 1847 and John Dunlop, 1887

There are many cases where original inventions have been abandoned, only for other people to re-invent the same concept later and rise to fame as a result. Scotsman Robert Thomson patented air-filled 'pneumatic' tyres in 1847, forty years before John Dunlop fitted rubber inner tubes to his son's tricycle wheels. While Thomson became frustrated with his leather-skinned tyre design, and ended up concentrating on solid rubber tyres for the steam wagons he developed, Dunlop's re-invention and persistence meant his name became one of the most widely recognized brands in the world. What a let down.

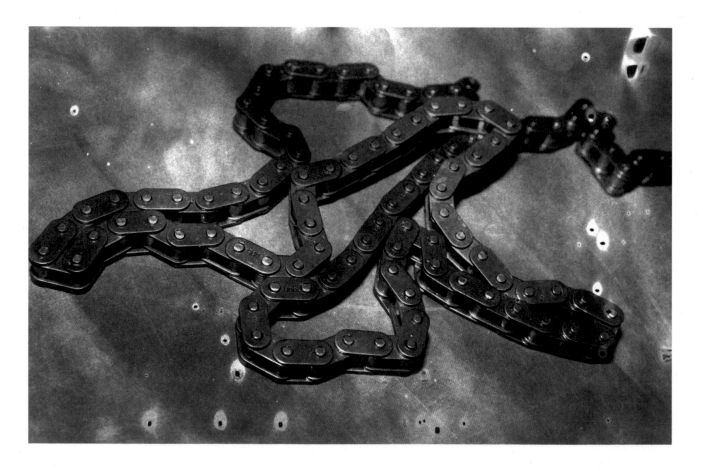

GREAT BRITISH INGENUITY

ELECTRIC AUTOMATIC KETTLE
BILL RUSSELL AND PETER HOBBS, 1955

For a nation obsessed with boiled water beverages it's perhaps surprising that the details of the origins of electric kettles are clouded in steam. The Swan company can definitely be credited with improving efficiency via the first submerged element kettle in 1922, but it was Bill Russell and Peter Hobbs who really turned everyone onto plug-in convenience and safety. As well as inventing the first coffee percolator, their K1 kettle was the first to use an automatic steam-sensing off switch, immediately leaving traditional stovetop kettles whistling in its wake. Tea-riffic.

It's not always megalomaniac momentum that creates world-changing ideas though, sometimes it's just simple necessity. Percy Shaw created the cat's eye reflective road marker when the tramlines that guided him along his local roads at night were removed. Tim Berners-Lee created the World Wide Web from already existing but unconnected protocols just so he could communicate and co-ordinate with his colleagues at the CERN laboratories more easily. While Owen Maclaren designed the undercarriage for the Spitfire, it is the folding aluminium-tubed baby buggy that he designed to stop his daughter struggling in and out of a conventional pram that he's best remembered for. It was leather-worker John Boultbee Brooks's horse folding up underneath him that forced him onto a wooden-seated bike and provided the kick in the arse needed to develop his own revolutionary saddle design; a design so perfect that even among the incredible list of British innovations whose stories we've told here, it's the only one that's still used and loved worldwide in an essentially unchanged form 151 years after John left home to set up his business with just £20 in his pocket.

CANNED FOOD
BRYAN DONKIN, 1811

While Napoleon launched the first competition to provide mass-produced preserved food, it was the British Army and Royal Navy who marched and sailed out across the Empire fuelled by beef and pea soup, and other moveable feasts, in large handmade tins from Donkin, Hall and Gamble.

REFLECTING TELESCOPE
ISAAC NEWTON, 1668

Gravity guru Isaac Newton revolutionized telescopes by bouncing their magnified images off a mirror and through a perpendicular eye piece. That solved colour diffraction disturbance, made the objective mirror easy to see and opened the way for much bigger, more powerful 'scopes.

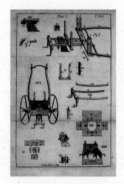

SEED DRILL
JETHRO TULL, 1701

The only inventor here to have a reasonably successful rock band named after him, Jethro Tull was very much into cutting grooves himself. He just used a horse-drawn drill to cut grooves in fields, drop neat rows of seeds in and then cover them up.

ROLLER BEARING
JOHN HARRISON, 1740

It took decades for Wakefield carpenter and clockmaker John Harrison to develop the sea clocks that eventually revolutionized maritime navigation. Buried deep in the doomed No. 3 clock were both the world's first friction-minimizing roller bearing and the first thermally sensitive bi-metallic strip. Not a total clock-up then.

MARINE CHRONOMETER
JOHN HARRISON, 1759

'Less is more' even applies to invention sometimes. John Harrison started developing his large sea clocks in 1730, but it wasn't until 1753 that he realized

that a smaller 130 mm diameter pocket watch format would work much better. Even that took six years to build and two years to test before it went on it's first voyage though.

MECHANIZED LOOM
JOHN KAY, JAMES HARGREAVES,
SAMUEL COMPTON 1738–79

It seems appropriate that the fully mechanized loom was woven from the ideas of several inventors. John Kay developed the speed-doubling fly shuttle, James Hargreaves's Spinning Jenny added multiple spindles and Samuel Compton's mechanized Spinning Mule created the yarn that fed into them.

THE MODERN FACTORY
RICHARD ARKWRIGHT, 1768

Richard Arkwright not only started powering his spinning machines from a water mill, he also built a purpose-designed mill at Cromford in Derbyshire to house them. As the machines didn't have to stop, Arkwright also introduced the idea of timed shifts for the workers and built a village for them so they didn't have to travel far.

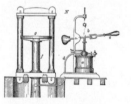

HYDRAULIC PRESS
JOSEPH BRAMAH, 1795

While Barnsley locksmith Joseph Bramah invented the force-multiplying hydraulic press to help create better locks, you're more likely to toast his ingenuity through his 'beer engine' design that still fills pints at most bars today.

STEAM LOCOMOTIVE
RICHARD TREVITHICK, 1801

We're not sure which bit we like most about Trevithick's terrific steam loco story: the fact that he developed his revolutionary high-pressure steam engine at the 'Ding Dong' tin mine, that he called the self-propelled version the 'Puffing Devil', or that it cooked its own goose when it caught fire while the driver was eating Christmas dinner.

FIXED WING FLIGHT
GEORGE CAYLEY, 1804

Some people devote their whole lives to creating one innovation, while others have more hot ideas than hot dinners. Yorkshire gent Sir George Cayley not only theorized all the vital aerodynamic elements (lift, drag, thrust and weight) while still at school, but also proved them; by 1804 he was flying his servants across a local valley in gliders complete with dihedral wings for stability and adjustable steering tailplanes.

TENSION-SPOKED WHEEL
GEORGE CAYLEY, 1808

Cayley didn't just assure smooth take-off of his gliders; they landed smoothly too, on the first tension-spoked wheels ever built. Not content with that, he also introduced the world to self-righting lifeboats, caterpillar tracks, seat belts and a spring-powered helicopter with metal rotors. Oh and his combustion engine would have pre-dated Daimler's engines by nearly a century had he replaced his gunpowder-powered original with petrol. Clearly an explosive intellect.

MODERN FIRE EXTINGUISHER
GEORGE WILLIAM MANBY, 1813

Few inventors have followed a more noble, helpful path than George Manby, who developed the ship safety-line firing 'Manby mortar', the compressed-air and potassium-carbonate charged 'Extincteur' fire extinguisher and advocated for the creation of a national fire brigade and lifeboat service.

ELECTRIC MOTOR
MICHAEL FARADAY, 1821

Faraday truly electrified science in the 19th century through his study and harnessing of electromagnetic forces. Not only did he put the world in a spin with his electromagnetic rotary motor, he also established the magnetic light-bending properties that would lead to TV.

WATERPROOF MATERIAL
CHARLES MACINTOSH, 1823

It's fair to say the Scottish get more weather than most, so perhaps it's no surprise that it was a Glaswegian chemist that first bonded a sandwich of fabric together with natural rubber. If only they'd got the spelling right when Mackintosh became a household name.

PORTLAND CEMENT
JOSEPH ASPDIN, 1824

Limestone-based building render had been around for centuries, but it was a Leeds bricklayer who refined a grinding, slaking and double-burning process that made it a strong, smooth and mouldable alternative to the finest Portland stone.

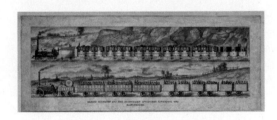

PASSENGER RAILWAY
GEORGE STEPHENSON, 1825

Self-taught steam pioneer 'Geordie' George Stephenson was building colliery engines from 1814, but it wasn't until 1825 that his Locomotion engine hauled the first passengers along the Stockton and Darlington railway. Because the carriage he built could also be horse-drawn it used the same 1422mm cartwheel gauge first seen in the Bronze Age and still in use on railways today.

LAWNMOWER
EDWIN BEARD BUDDING, 1827

Yes, it's his fault. Budding's bladed-reel lawnmower upsized designs used for smoothing woollen cloth to curse every summer suburban weekend with the hayfever-haters chore, and sideline the scythe for everyone but the Grim Reaper.

PHOTOGRAPHY
WILLIAM HENRY FOX TALBOT, 1835

Louis Daguerre might have given his name to the daguerreotype in 1839, but Talbot was producing 'salted paper' images four years earlier. Naming his translucent negative, multiple-reproduction development 'Talbotyping' didn't stick either, but 'calotyping', as it became known, did get him a medal from the Royal Society.

ELECTRIC TELEGRAPH
CHARLES WHEATSTONE
AND WILLIAM COOKE, 1837

Who says crime doesn't pay? Despite being developed and refined for eight years previously, it was a telegraph message securing the arrest of murderer John Tawell that put it into the limelight. Ironically, it was lack of communication that created a bitter feud between the two inventors.

CHOCOLATE BAR
JS FRY & SONS, 1847

Sometimes everything you need for a world-changing invention has been under your nose for ages without you realizing it. The Fry family had been making and selling chocolate for eighty-eight years before Joseph Fry managed to press a mix of cocoa powder, sugar and cocoa together to create the first chocolate bar. Nineteen years later he added a fondant centre to create the soft-centre Chocolate Cream, and he rolled out the first chocolate Easter egg in 1873. Sweet work, Joseph.

SYNTHETIC DYE
WILLIAM PERKIN, 1856

Eager young inventor Bill Perkin was trying to synthesize quinine (later adopted as a treatment for malaria) from toxic aniline when he accidentally created an intense purple colourant he called mauveine. In other words, he didn't stop people dying, but he did start people dyeing.

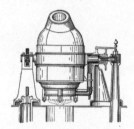

BESSEMER PROCESS
HENRY BESSEMER, 1856

Henry Bessemer was the first to blow oxygen through molten pig iron and then add carbon in order to help blow people up (as the much purer steel this process created was originally intended for gun manufacture). This purer steel, with its linked rolling process, replaced engineering iron everywhere, from bridges and buildings to railways and ships.

LINOLEUM
FREDERICK WALTON, 1860

Fred Walton first skimmed the skin off linseed oil to see if it would work as a rubber substitute. He only found a solid commercial footing once he mixed the linseed varnish with cork and timber dust and framed it on a cloth backing to create tough, decorative Lino.

SEWAGE SYSTEM
JOSEPH BAZALGETTE, 1865

London's sewage system was first created by the Romans, but the infamous 'Great Stink' of 1858 and cholera outbreaks confirmed what a shit state London was in. Bazalgette used a multi-level network of sewers to flush the problem eastwards, away from the city, creating a system still in rude health today.

MODERN TORPEDO
ROBERT WHITEHEAD, 1866

Lancashire inventor Robert Whitehead was actually working in Austria when he developed his self-propelled compressed air engine, hydrostatic levelling device and gyroscopic guidance 'Torpedo'. It quickly evolved into a revolutionary weapon, while his daughter Alice quickly eloped with the captain of the ship used to test it.

STAINLESS STEEL
JOHN CLARK AND JOHN T. WOODS, 1872

While English metallurgical mates Clark and Woods developed their low-carbon, high-chromium iron alloy in 1872, the name 'stainless steel' wasn't widely adopted for such metals until fifty years later. It only became viable for bike-building in the past decade.

TELEPHONE
ALEXANDER GRAHAM BELL, 1876

Bell was a third-generation speech and elocution specialist with a deaf wife and mother and it was this experience that led him to develop the first telephone. He actually refused to have such a distracting device in his study during his subsequent hydrofoil, aeronautical and *National Geographic*-developing career.

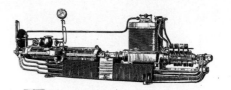

STEAM TURBINE
CHARLES PARSONS, 1884

After thirteen years of development, Charles Parsons ran rings round the Royal Navy at Queen Victoria's Diamond Jubilee fleet in 1897 to prove just how powerful and efficient his multi-phase steam turbines were. In under a decade his engines were powering the *Dreadnought*, the fastest and most powerful battleship in the navy.

ROVER SAFETY BICYCLE
JOHN KEMP STARLEY, 1885

Various treadle- and chain-powered small-wheel bikes had already tried to topple the dominant monster-wheel 'Ordinary' bikes of the late 19th century. It was Starley who combined easy ground reach, effective braking and efficient drive in his Rover model to make 'Safety Bikes' an extraordinary commercial success.

THERMOS FLASK
SIR JAMES DEWAR, 1892

James Dewar might have invented the vacuum flask to store liquid gases for observation, but most of us use it to keep our drinks hot. Similarly perversely, while scientists still use the term Dewar flask, the design was cheekily patented by two German glassblowers under the Thermos brand.

FOUR-WHEEL DRIVE
BRAMAH DIPLOCK, 1893

Bramah's revolutionary all-terrain traction engine not only had four-wheel drive, it also had four-wheel steering and his radical foot-equipped 'Pedrail' wheels to reduce ground pressure and increase traction. It had three differential gears, but we don't know if Diplock had diff lock.

ELECTRIC VACUUM CLEANER
HUBERT CECIL BOOTH, 1901

Booth tested his idea for a hygienic dust remover by unhygienically sucking air into his mouth through a handkerchief placed on a restaurant chair. Surviving that, he set about building a fleet of horse-drawn vacuum cleaners using suction tubes fed in through the windows of buildings, before developing his more convenient domestic 'Goblin'.

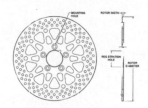

DISC BRAKES
FREDERICK WILLIAM LANCHESTER, 1902

English car pioneer Lanchester didn't just create the first wick carburettor and epicyclic gearbox for automobile use, he also fitted the first disc brakes in 1901. It worked on the engine shaft, but not the wheels, and with an inefficient worm drive transmission and boat-style tiller rather than steering wheel it was a curious beast to drive.

MILITARY TANK
LT COLONEL ERNEST SWINTON, 1914

Leonardo da Vinci drew one and H.G. Wells wrote stories about them, but it was Ernest Swinton who was tasked with turning tracked farm machines into trench-crossing weapons. He also coined the term 'tank' to mislead spies from the true intentions behind the big armoured boxes he was developing, though why the first one was called 'Little Willie' is more of a mystery.

AUTOMATIC WATCH
JOHN HARWOOD, 1923

John Harwood loved making automatic things. He'd already made an automatic pistol and an impact-driven screwdriver while working as an armoury sergeant before launching his Harwood Perpetual watch. The design is still used today, although unfortunately Harwood had to wind up his own company in 1931.

TELEVISION
JOHN LOGIE BAIRD, 1925

Baird was a truly eccentric inventor using an old hatbox, a pair of scissors, darning needles and lenses from bike lights to create his first moving pictures of a ventriloquist's dummy. His claims of 'seeing by wireless' even got him thrown out of the *Daily Express* offices 'as a lunatic who might have a razor on him'.

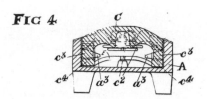

CAT'S EYE
PERCY SHAW, 1933

Percy Shaw was already working as a road contractor when his often meandering, night-time drive between a Yorkshire pub and home led him to develop his revolutionary self-cleaning 'Cat's Eye' road studs.

JET ENGINE
SIR FRANK WHITTLE, 1937

Renowned acrobatic reprobate and engineering genius Frank Whittle theorized his turbojet in the 1920s, but continued Air Ministry indifference meant that the WU engine didn't roar into action until 1937. Whittle had already had a nervous breakdown over the delays before his first engine left the ground in 1941.

ELECTRONIC PROGRAMMABLE COMPUTER
TOMMY FLOWERS, 1943

Flowers started working in electronic communications at the General Post Office, rapidly moving into the Research & Development department before becoming involved in automating the code-breaking process of the Bletchley Park boffins. His resulting Colossus was the first programmable, pattern-generating electronic computer using over ten times as many valves than its predecessor.

HOVERCRAFT
CHRISTOPHER COCKERELL, 1953

Business at Christopher Cockerell's small boat and caravan hire company got the literal lift it needed when he used a fan engine to blow into a skirt dangling below a boat's hull to create the first hovercraft.

FLOAT GLASS
ALASTAIR PILKINGTON, 1957

Steel innovator Henry Bessemer was the first to roll sheets of glass, but it was another 110 years before the Pilkington brothers perfected flowing a precise volume of molten glass over a bath of molten tin in a 90% nitrogen atmosphere to create perfect sheets of amazing glazing.

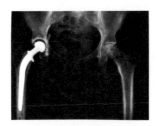

HIP REPLACEMENT
JOHN CHARNLEY, 1959

Sometimes it takes a lot of small steps to make giant strides. John Charnley worked as a surgeon for many years before finally fitting his first PTFE-coated hip replacement in 1959. Even then it was a long time before improved surgical hygiene and polyethylene coatings made the process consistently successful though.

CARBON FIBRE
ROYAL AIRCRAFT ESTABLISHMENT ENGINEERS, 1963

Various firms and engineers had been working on increasingly high-performance carbon fibres, but it was the boffins at Farnborough who created the first aerospace-quality composites. UK brand Carlton developed the first composite tubed bike in 1971.

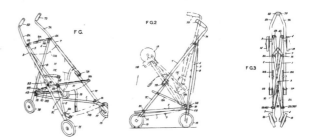

COLLAPSIBLE BABY BUGGY
OWEN MACLAREN, 1965

Owen Maclaren designed the Spitfire's undercarriage, but it was his lightweight, collapsible stroller that made him a household name. 'We shall fold them on the beaches, we shall fold them on the landing grounds, we shall fold them in the fields and the streets', as Churchill might have said…

ATM
JOHN SHEPHERD-BARRON, 1967

The first cash machine was developed by Barron's firm De La Rue and installed in Barclays Bank, Enfield. The original design used paper cheques issued by the bank cashier though, with PIN pads only added later.

WORLD WIDE WEB
TIM BERNERS-LEE, 1989

Most modern inventions are buried in patents and legal restrictions, but the whole idea behind Tim Berners-Lee's creation of the World Wide Web was to extend it globally, so he didn't impose any patents or royalties on it. Thanks Tim.

WIND-UP RADIO
TREVOR BAYLIS, 1991

Howard Stern might be the master of winding people up on the radio, but it was Englishman Trevor Baylis who designed a clockwork radio for improving health communication in AIDS-stricken Africa. Subsequent models included emergency sirens and torches too.

RON ARAD

Industrial designer, artist and
architect, photographed at his studio
in Camden Town

BRITAIN IS A GOOD PLACE FOR A DESIGN EDUCATION. When I was teaching I'd say I wanted to make students 'unemployable' mostly to scare Christopher Frayling, the Rector at the Royal College of Art. People can find jobs, but the whole idea was to plant an appetite in students to *not* be part of that army of employees, but to do something else: to be different. We never used the word 'should'. You know, 'this should be like this' or 'this should be like that'.

Oscar Wilde defined art as something that has no function. I don't agree with that; I don't agree with anything that's prescriptive. Ettore Sottsass, the founder of Memphis [Italian design group], once said 'money is very jealous, if you ignore it, it will run after you...'. That was an OK sentence to bear in mind. I always saw the Business as a necessary evil. I didn't design for the business, but the business supported the work, not the other way round. When I took over at the Royal College it was, 'good design is good business' slogans, and people thought the way to justify an art school was with the economy.

The fact is I came here in '73, and I didn't come here to stay, but I did stay. There wasn't a design industry here then. I had to invent my own profession. And that forced me to make stuff. I didn't have a five-year plan to become a designer, I just did things. In the early '80s there was a sort of street culture in London and experimentation, and new cultural magazines like

The Face or *Blueprint*. When we watch videos of parties at the studio from then, it was a happy, wild time; we didn't know any better.

There are a lot of things you have to admire about Britain. There was a vote in the police force to decide whether they should be armed or not, and 80% voted not to be armed. I can't think of any other place in the world where police would vote to *not* be given guns. That is absolutely amazing. It is quite a liberal place, even if we see a Conservative government. We used to twitch when Margaret Thatcher would say 'we are a very tolerant nation'. Which meant there's a lot to tolerate. There are some things where you say 'ooh that's very British' and then there's the opposite that can also be described as British. There's not one thing that is British. There's one thing and its opposite. That couldn't be better demonstrated by the last [EU] referendum.

I'm a city man and an island man: for escape I go to Spain, to a little island. When I was first introduced to this island by the artist Javier Mariscal he described the island beautifully, and drew a map and all this, and then he said, 'but there's no saxophones on the island.' I said 'Sorry? No saxophones? What do you mean?' And he said, 'there's Italians, French people, Germans, but no saxophones.' Of course, he meant no Anglo-Saxons. But he was wrong, there were Anglo-Saxons on the island, and every time I saw a Brit there I'd say, 'Oh look, a saxophone.'

FRANK HERHOLDT

Advertising photographer,
photographed at his home
in Bethnal Green

I'VE LIVED IN THE UK SINCE 1984. I'm originally from Johannesburg, but this was the first time I'd seen inside anything so Victorian. I grew up in the apartheid era, a Fascist state, where people were shot in the street for protesting. I saw things a child shouldn't see. I was arrested for dancing with a black girl in a black club. When I got to London I was so grateful, it drove me on. I was just thrilled to be here, to be able to read the free press, and to see the tolerance of different cultures – the open-mindedness. It's a place where new things can happen. I've just always loved the UK, I feel very privileged to be here. When you see the school my kids go to, these children skip to school. When I went to school I was beaten and used to be really unhappy. At my kids' school they close for Eid and Christmas. There are Bangladeshi parents, Italian parents, gay parents. And all these children play happily together. It's a great situation.

I came from South Africa to London as a photographer, and was lucky enough to get jobs assisting some really good photographers, like Lester Bookbinder and Michael Joseph. One of the first jobs we did was for Rolls-Royce, which we shot under a walnut tree (because of the walnut dash in the car) in this muddy field. At the time that was very revolutionary. And for Mercedes-Benz we photographed scientists in a rapeseed field in Scotland. In those days they'd give you three days to get one shot.

A lot of my first jobs in the UK were failures; it affected my confidence. And that drove me on. I used it as a tool. There was no way I would go back to J'burg with my tail between my legs. The fear of failure pushed me, and made me more experimental. And I came up with the idea of using movie lighting for my shoots. But my work continuously changes. In Britain I think there's a really high standard of photography, terrifyingly good actually, the amount of talent. But at the same time maybe some of the technical skill is falling away. The main thing about photography really is being able to understand light and use light in an interesting way.

The business is tough and competitive here. But that's what keeps you going, being confronted with challenges.

MADE IN BRITAIN

BEN WILSON

Designer and maker, photographed
by Jens Marrot at his workshop
in East London

I LOVE THE WAY WE TAKE THE OLD AND MASH IT UP with more contemporary ideas. [My brother Oscar and I] did a white leather Brooks saddle in collaboration with Californian brand Stüssy. At the time it was quite a different thing to do for an old-school company like Brooks. I'm very into music; if you think of the sampler and how that changed a lot of things, you see that in Britain that is done with all sorts – repurposing elements into something new. I remember when we were kids our dad taking us to see Malcolm McLaren exhibitions and then to watch BMX racing. We were sponges for everything. And that has helped us join the dots between lots of things.

I think that get-up-and-go and make-it-happen mentality, even if you're not an expert, that DIY thing, I guess that's quite a British trait. It's a kind of entrepreneurialism. We make the most with what we've got: how can we get the best out of the brief with our time, money and creativity? How do you find that sweet spot? You have to innovate. We don't conform that much. As a design duo we've been lucky to have a very uncalculated journey so far. We did a project for Nike, and we were so naive to architecture and interior design, but I think that helped because we did it differently. It was more a feeling about what was right at the time.

I initially trained in craft, then went to the Royal College of Art to do an MA in product and industrial design, studying under Ron Arad. Ron Arad would say, 'I take students who are perfectly employable and make them unemployable…'. They (his students) make their own way of thinking and working. It doesn't get boring, particularly working in London, it offers a lot of opportunity. There are lots of different people from lots of different backgrounds, it's very stimulating and inspiring. But it's also hard in London: you've got to pedal hard or you won't even get off the starting block. But that makes it competitive, it makes you strive to be different. Take for example the question of 'what is luxury?' A well-built bicycle is a much more efficient way of travelling around London than a Lamborghini.

We work with bikes a lot and cycling has always been a big influence on our work: I was lucky to be brought up on a BMX by my dad, and building ramps and bikes from different parts is probably how I learnt about engineering and geometry. What's not to like about bikes? You put in a bit and you get a lot out. They're good for you and they make you feel good.

SIMON MOTTRAM

Founder and CEO of Rapha,
photographed at his home in London

MADE IN BRITAIN

BRITAIN IS AN ISLAND, so we haven't been invaded (too much) in the past and successfully built trade and manufacturing wealth with the Empire, being first to the table with industrialization. But I think the failure and decline of 'Great Britain' as an empire in the 20th century was actually a really powerful creative driver. That sense of loss perhaps gave us this rush of ideas, that creative spark.

Just because we've been making things for a long time doesn't mean we're any good at manufacturing. I think there's a difference between 'made' in Britain and 'designed' in Britain. Most people can make things very well; know-how and physicality can be replicated anywhere in the world. But 'designed in Britain', that's more interesting to me.

This island is certainly a bit angry, and slightly mad – full of mad scientists and left-field eccentricity, leading to amazing contraptions and ideas (look at James Dyson and Trevor Bayliss). But those kind of garden-shed inventors don't really appeal to me.

Rapha is very much based on continental culture, but with our own twist. We're not called 'Arkwright' [the Rapha name has its roots in French cycle racing], we like sun-drenched mountain stages at the Tour rather than time trials on damp roads.

I like going to Japan because there's a creative tension that I see in Britain as well. They had an empire too, and are very proud – there's a dignity there; they are very industrious, and are intensely devoted to whatever they focus on. And like us in Britain, they want authenticity, but are also quite playful with things. The British and the Japanese are both good at grabbing ideas from other places, magpie-like, taking a tradition or style and reinterpreting it. We bend the rules. And I think that also has something to do with the (bad) food and weather, in Britain at least.

I think there's a strong sense of non-conformity in the UK; look at punk, for example: punk would never have started in mainland Europe. The conditions in NYC and London in the 1970s – racial tension, alienation, class war, recession – created a reaction against what came before … It's that frustration and anger which makes it more daring, and it has an edge to it, because things aren't perfect. It's the confidence to be different, and the inventiveness that comes from asking questions.

RICHARD WENTWORTH

Artist and teacher photographed
at the Science Museum

I LOVE THE FACT THAT THE V-2 ROCKET DOESN'T QUITE FIT. There is a plane in here, the chrome Vickers, that transported Neville Chamberlain back from his meeting with Adolf Hitler in 1938. That conference was a catalyst for war. Science is politics.

I think that we [Britain] had the easiest-to-mine coal in the world, and of course the steam engine and combustion, and then the 'colonies' for resources. British inventiveness has something to do with an obsession with materials – whether you are an artist or an engineer, you want to make things. Like art, technology is influenced by lots of things; the Lumière brothers got the idea for their cinema projector from a sewing machine!

I think the British like to tinker. Look at James Watt's workshop [a replica is housed in the Science Museum] – he was a champion fiddler; a bit like a cobbler making shoes. That mentality comes out of being adjacent to lots of other thinkers, meeting in coffee shops in the 18th century [in Watt's case at Soho House in Handsworth, Birmingham] and saying 'the weirdest thing happened!' Ideas that were very 'punk', you know, just do it yourself (DIY). My son Joe, he used to build robots ... Not humanoid Japanese 'tin-men', but ones you could control to destroy other robots. Living on an island certainly creates individuals with a need to reinterpret, continuously rethinking things. Also, being ignorant to something can make you more curious about it, and therefore more creative.

This country is an absorber: we had coal and steam, but not much else, so we had to be inventive. So with all of the trade and commerce the UK was involved in – lots of ideas and values from all over the world came in. And the world is at its most interesting when people talk to each other ... The Great Exhibition of 1851 brought shedloads of money into London, which built these museums ... All that stuff about nationhood was invented around that time (we didn't need passports before 1918) and it combined with this boom in manufacturing, so countries became associated with their particular industries and the products they made.

TIMOTHY EVEREST

Tailor, photographed outside
his premises in Spitalfields

IN BRITAIN WE VALUE INDIVIDUALITY IMMENSELY, and we're constantly looking for new things. There's a magpie-like approach that sets the Brits apart. It goes back to the Empire and exploration, like finding exotic teas and adding milk and sugar. I often think about a discussion I witnessed in Italy, or rather an argument, over where the best pizza was from: so you had a guy from Naples talking about having the sweetest tomatoes and creamiest mozzarella, and someone from Rome arguing about the thickness of the base, going into real depth about something so simple. In England the conversation would be very different; you'd talk about which new restaurant to go to… So perhaps we're more outwards looking, not happy with what already exists. I think Brits want to understand the wider world they inhabit. We're constantly worrying about the past and looking at the future, and we're not very good at living in the present. We reference history but try to find new ways of doing things. But not everything is new, it's just a different view or interpretation. Rethinking things. Music is a good example; we have had the same notes for a very long time, but different ways of playing them come and go.

It's very interesting at the moment in the UK. I believe we've been in a golden era, with events such as the royal wedding, the Olympics, the Silver Jubilee. There's been a big focus on Britain, the likes of which we've not seen since the 1960s.

As a tailor I'm very interested in the craft and Savile Row sensibility, of course. We [Timothy Everest] select traditional elements and techniques from the past – colour, fit, cut – but we then bring them up to date. Bespoke tailoring in London is rather unique. I was lucky in a way: I got a job in Savile Row in my teens, having wanted to work in fashion, then I met Tommy Nutter and went to work for him, designing for people such as Elton John and Jack Nicholson. It was going right up to the top level, the equivalent of Formula 1 or the (English football) Premiership. It was based on honouring the rules of the tailoring tradition, but subverting them. People just wanted great suits. I think also Paul Smith and the success he has had gave a lot of British designers permission to be more creative. We take influences from all over at Timothy Everest, but we always come back to a certain British style and attitude that is admired around the world.

CAREN HARTLEY

Frame builder at Hartley Cycles,
photographed at her workshop
in Peckham

I THINK THERE IS OFTEN A SUBTLE SENSE OF HUMOUR EVIDENT in British design, and maybe the feeling that the designers aren't afraid to approach things in the 'wrong' way and experiment with new methods, even developing completely new making techniques in the process. I think there is also a lot of cross-pollination across the different craft, design and art disciplines, with makers 'borrowing' techniques and materials from each other.

I trained in 3D design and metalwork and had been working as a sculptor and also a jeweller for a number of years (there's a huge handmade jewelry industry in the UK, and many of my friends are jewellers selling worldwide), but it wasn't until I moved to London that I really got into cycling and bikes and then, after gradually becoming more and more immersed in the cycling community, I started to think about using my skills to create a more useful type of object – the bicycle. Being one of the few women doing this meant that I stood out, which was useful, especially in the early stages of Hartley Cycles. But that extra attention can mean a lot of pressure and the feeling of having to prove myself, perhaps more than my male counterparts. One of the most frequently asked questions I got at the start was, 'So, who does your welding?!'

I take influences from all over the place; it might be a theme that I've developed from something a customer likes, such as the Rolls-Royce Phantom, or maps of an area. Or it might be things other designers are doing with colour or texture. And then there are shapes and forms that I keep coming back to – I love the Art Deco and Modernist periods and the shapes and proportions found in objects, buildings and graphics from these eras are something I revisit often.

It was really the British cycling community that lured me into becoming a frame builder though. The cycling industry and bespoke craft industries alike are very welcoming and supportive, and there's the feeling that everyone in it wants everyone else to do well – we're all in it together against mass production.

WILL BUTLER-ADAMS

CEO of Brompton Bicycles,
photographed on the shop floor
in Greenford

BROMPTON'S INVENTOR [ANDREW RITCHIE] RENTED A FLAT on the Cromwell Road that overlooks the Brompton Oratory, hence the name. He started the company in a railway arch in Brentford with an Irish brazier called Paddy. As we grew we could have moved out of London, and even the UK, but we would have lost what we're about. We make a folding bike that 70% of our staff use, because it makes sense if you live in London. But if we weren't using the thing, what's the point? For us, it is the confidence to have clarity about what we do; in our case, it is that form follows function.

We want to create the best value, the most efficient, the best bike we can sell, so we combine cutting-edge technology and traditional brazing. We do all our brazing here – every single Brompton is made in the UK. People come in here and start as pickers, then might move into working on the CNC machine, and then they either go into assembly or brazing. Engineering isn't boring – if you go to Google HQ everyone looks trendy and sits around on bean-bags, but it's really a boring job, dealing with programming all day. Our job here is actually very cool – we make stuff.

Our customers aren't cyclists, they're urbanites. I spend a lot of time pedalling around cities all over the world. It has been estimated that by 2050, 60% of the world's population will be living in cities. The average journey to work is four miles in London, yet people are still coming down in the lift of their building, going straight into a hole in the ground and squashing into a tiny space to travel to work. So we need to make cities more liveable places again, and there's a massive place for bikes and technology in that.

I'm deeply proud of being British, but I don't think people buy Bromptons because we're British. The flag is irrelevant, it's the product that needs to be the best, and that's the Britishness: it's more innovative, it's a more delightful product. We're quite different because all we do is make a Brompton, so we are perfectionists. All the engineered jigs, our machinery, the way the work flows, all that is adding value to the product.

People get caught up in doing what they think is right, following a crowd. And the British are good at saying, 'Hold on, what on earth are they doing that for? This makes more sense.' If you drive your own furrow and have the confidence to be 'odd' or 'different', that's how you innovate. It's the Brits that have always been good at questioning; take Darwin's theory of evolution, he wasn't following the crowd. When I was at school we spent most of our time trying to break the rules, and that's a British thing. We want to be different; dancing around with funny little sticks and bells on our ankles. I tell my staff, 'disrupt and cause problems', because from disorder, you discover things.

SIR PAUL SMITH

Designer, photographed in his
offices in Covent Garden

IT ALL STARTED WITH THE COPPER RIVETS ... I got my first road bike at the age of twelve, in the late 1950s. During the 1960s riders were into customizing things, like drilling holes in brake levers and the soles of their shoes. There was also this thing for adding copper rivets to your Brooks saddle. A pal of mine in the cycle club I belonged to would bash the original rivets out and put copper ones in, and get this lovely finish on them. It's those details you find on a bike that are so attractive, like the fluting on a Campagnolo seat pillar.

That knack for tinkering with things is very British. I work with John Lobb, the shoemaker, and when you go to their factory in Northampton, the guys working on the shoes there have all these nails in their mouth, hammering each one at a time, and they don't miss; it's this beautiful, artisan skill.

The UK is a country that is full of very inventive people. My father had a darkroom in our attic that you used a ladder on a homemade pulley system to get up into. I'd sit there with him printing pictures he'd taken. He loved putting two pictures together, including a print of me flying a magic carpet over Brighton pier! The interest in the world and the creativity, the inventiveness that he had comes from a curious mind, always asking questions. Yet when I told my dad – after I left school at fifteen – that I wanted to be a bike racer he said: 'That's not a proper job, son...'.

But until the age of seventeen I only thought about being a bike rider. Then I crashed badly, and the injury stopped me racing. I met these art students in the pub who taught me about strange things called 'Bauhaus' and 'Kandinsky'... I soon realized I could use inventiveness to make a living.

CROSS CONTAMINATIONS

Amy Sherlock

It is often said that the earliest known sketch of a bicycle is by Leonardo da Vinci, discovered while the *Codex Atlanticus* – the largest compilation of his notes and drawings – was being restored in the late 1960s. The veracity of this claim has been debated by academics and historians for decades; now widely discredited, it seems likely the sketch was the invention of a much later forger, who took creative liberties with two existing sketches of circles bisected by lines.

If the bicycle's pleasing geometries – triangles, circles, arcs – lend themselves to incorporation in pieces of art or design, this formal appeal is matched by its rich and varied symbolism. As a cipher for mobility, emancipation, equality, industry, ecology – among other things – the bicycle has found its way into the arts as a means of reflecting on some of the most pressing social and cultural issues of the day.

The persistence of the Leonardo origin myth says something about the romanticization of the bicycle in contemporary culture. In truth, the story of its development goes hand in hand with that of industrialization: in terms both of the technologies of its manufacture and because it was, for many years and in many societies worldwide, the principal means of transporting workers to and from factories. In the early 20th century, the economic, political and cultural upheavals ushered in by industrialization and urbanization led writers and artists to new forms of expression intended to convey the pace of contemporary life and the fractured sense of self it produced. The bicycle began to appear in the work of the European artistic avant-gardes as a harbinger of the emancipated 'modern' subject, and hopeful symbol of our mechanized future.

Following the volatile start to the 20th century and through the devastation of the World Wars, the bicycle took on a more ambivalent significance – of futility and mortality, or a quixotic longing to return to earlier, simpler times. Hence Picasso mounts a pair of old rusty handlebars above a worn leather saddle and invests it with the magical, spiritual dimension of a tribal totem; Duchamp watches a bicycle wheel go around and around and around until it slows to a stop. More recently, Lucy and Jorge Orta have used a cargo trike to carry clouds: a utopic proposal for stalling or circumventing the cycles of production and consumption that are leading humanity towards ecological disaster.

Potent images of human ingenuity as well as hubris, bicycles are pliable artistic material, both physically and symbolically.

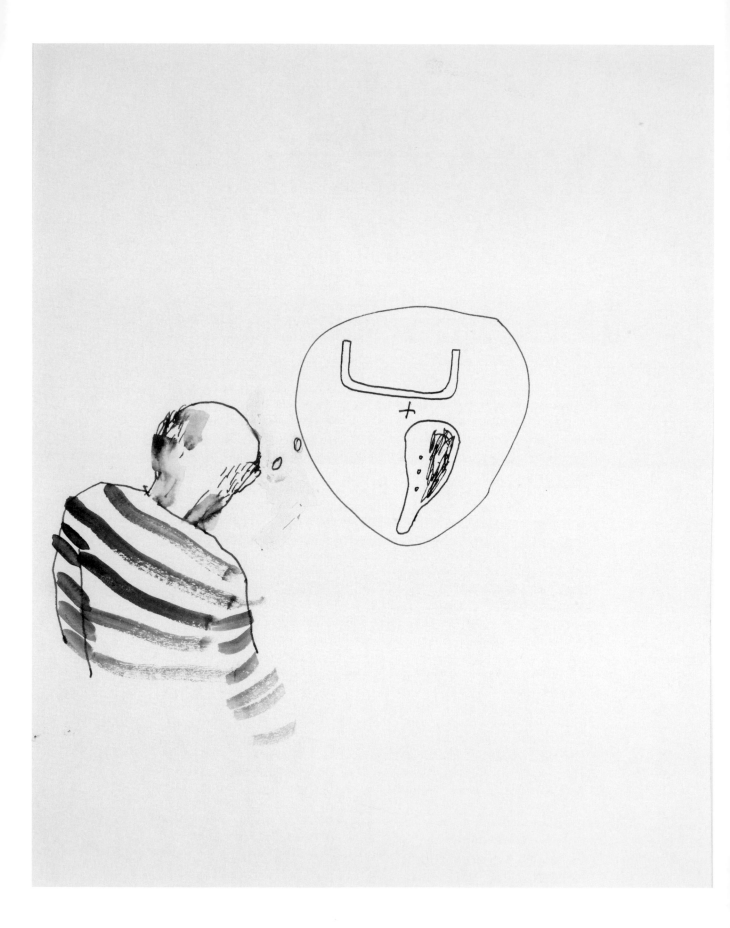

CROSS CONTAMINATIONS

PABLO PICASSO

Inspiration for *Bull's Head*, 1942

'Guess how I made the bull's head?' Pablo Picasso asked the photographer Brassaï, when the latter visited his studio in occupied Paris in 1943. In truth, the origins of the sculpture, assembled by Picasso the previous year, are not hard to guess. Take one bicycle seat, well worn, crown with an upturned pair of rusty handlebars *et voilà:* the gaunt apparition of a bull's head, angular and mysterious, like a cave painting or archaic totem. 'All I did was weld them together,' explained the Cubist master.

And yet, *Bull's Head* says more than Picasso lets on: the sculpture's very simplicity is a reminder of the deprivations of wartime Europe, its aged leather and rusty steel mourning garb for the lost era of carefree bicycle rides and the freedoms that two wheels embody. The work has a macabre cousin in the half-formed *Death's Head* of 1941, made in the early days of Paris's Nazi occupation – a pockmarked, hollow-eyed bronze whose scarred complexion queasily prefigures the burn victims of the bombs that would fall four years later on Hiroshima and Nagasaki.

But it's not all darkness: there is a wry humour to *Bull's Head*, whose powerful, shamanic form suggests the magical powers through which art can transform the mundane into the mystical. Marcel Duchamp, of course, had been pointing this out for years with his 'readymade' sculptures: found objects presented as works of art. In fact, we might even read Picasso's sculpture as a riposte to the very first of these, a bicycle wheel attached to a kitchen stool, which Duchamp made in 1913. The wheel goes round and round, turning but getting nowhere; Picasso's *Bull's Head* hangs like a big-game trophy, or perhaps a scalp – having beaten, on this occasion, the Dadaist wit at his own game.

UMBERTO BOCCIONI

Dynamism of a Cyclist, 1913

(previous pages)

MARCEL DUCHAMP

Bicycle Wheel, 1913

'We affirm that the beauty of the world has been enriched by a new form of beauty: the beauty of speed,' declared the first *Futurist Manifesto*, authored by the Italian poet Filippo Tommaso Marinetti and published in the French newspaper *Le Figaro* in February 1909. Decrying the torpor of Italy's museums and academies and their slavish study of the past, Futurism praised machines, engines and the 'cleansing' violence of war.

Futurist painter Umberto Boccioni's works draw heavily on the fractured, overlapping perspectives of Picasso's and Braque's early Cubist experiments to communicate the constant and discombobulating flux of contemporary existence. For Marinetti, the bicycle had a complicated relationship to his dreams of mechanization: infamously, his Futurist thinking was galvanized by an automobile accident in which he swerved into a ditch to avoid knocking down two cyclists. The frenzied brushwork of Boccioni's *Dynamism of a Cyclist* (1913), however, melds man and machine, with the bicycle becoming a kind of prosthesis, wheels as limbs for increased velocity.

When war was loosed in Europe in 1914, and Italy joined the fray in 1915, Marinetti enrolled in the Lombard Battalion of Volunteer Cyclists and was stationed, for a short time, on the Austrian front in the Alps above Lake Garda. However, in a twist that Marinetti, recalling his unfortunate roll in the ditch, might have found grimly satisfying, the unit was disbanded before the end of 1915, their antiquated equipment deemed unsuited to the realities of modern conflict. Marinetti retrained as an artilleryman and saw action in both World Wars. Boccioni was not so lucky: in a fateful reminder of old-fashioned dangers, he was thrown from his horse during cavalry exercises, in 1916, and died from his injuries.

Duchamp, for his part, gave an equally simple explanation of the genesis of the *Bicycle Wheel* to Picasso's musings on *Bull's Head*. In a 1961 talk at the Museum of Modern Art (MoMA), New York, he recalled: 'In 1913, I had the happy idea to fasten a bicycle wheel to a kitchen stool and watch it turn.' What could be more straightforwardly pleasing, almost childlike, than endless, hypnotic motion? (Duchamp once compared it to watching 'flames dancing in a fireplace'.) However, in bringing the mundane and mass-produced into the realm of high art, the artist had opened a Pandora's box from which Pop, Minimalism, Conceptualism and every other significant artistic movement of the second half of the 20th century would issue. An inveterate paronomasiac, Duchamp could hardly have been unaware of the double sense of the word 'revolution': a wheel fixed to a stool may go nowhere, but this one forever set art history along a different route.

The first *Bicycle Wheel* was lost when Duchamp moved from Paris to New York in 1915, as was a replacement made the following year. History does not relate whether different types of bicycle were used for each. What is known, however, is that when Duchamp came to make a third version, in 1951, for an exhibition, his New York gallerist Sydney Janis selected both components: the stool came from Brooklyn, while the seat had been acquired a year earlier in Paris. (Was Janis perhaps imagining the Tour de France peloton rolling into the velodrome at Parc des Princes?)

The 1951 version is now in the collection of the Museum of Modern Art. In a curious incident, in 1995, a man walked in off the street and took the wheel, escaping up Fifth Avenue in a taxi before security could catch up. It was returned a day later: unceremoniously dumped – as with so many stolen bicycles – over the wall into the Museum's garden.

Marcel Duchamp in his studio,
Neuilly-sur-Seine, France, 1968,
photographed by Henri Cartier-Bresson

CROSS CONTAMINATIONS

ACHILLE AND PIER GIACOMO CASTIGLIONI

Sella telephone stool, 1957

In the bottom left-hand corner of an early sketch of Achille Castiglioni's *Sella* stool is a simple line drawing of a bicycle seat topped by a set of handlebars: Pablo Picasso's *Bull's Head* sculpture. We might imagine the two pieces having a similar genesis: coming across an old bicycle seat amid the debris of the studio, one inventive mind gave us an iconic work of art, and the other an icon of design. They're twins, of sorts, not only in the use of the same 'readymade' component, but in a certain shared wit and economy of design.

Pivoting on a hemispheric base by means of a milkshake-pink, tubular stem, Castiglioni's seat was ostensibly designed as a stool on which to make calls from a payphone. The practical difficulties of transporting the object to and from a phone booth notwithstanding, *Sella* neatly evokes the fidgety optimism of the late 1950s when, after the difficult postwar years, Italian design was beginning to come into its own. (*Sella* itself did not go into production until 1981, around the time that the postmodern aesthetic it had, by some years, prefigured found its Baroque apogee, in the designs of Ettore Sottsass and the Memphis group.)

'There has to be irony both in design and in the objects,' Achille Castiglioni once said. 'I see around me a professional disease of taking everything too seriously. One of my secrets is to joke all the time.' Sentiments with which Picasso and Duchamp would surely agree.

CROSS CONTAMINATIONS

JEAN TINGUELY

Homage to New York, 1960

When a bicycle – in however mangled or dismembered a form – is introduced into a piece of art, it can't help but raise questions about use-value and function. (Could there ever be a non-functional bicycle? When art becomes useful, is it still art?) Duchamp made the transformation of working tools into works of art a kind of alchemy, turning wood and steel into gold. But, from the late 1950s, the Swiss sculptor Jean Tinguely took the absurdity and the pathos of the 'readymade' and amplified them through a series of banging, crashing mechanical contraptions that worked perfectly but served no purpose at all.

In *Cyclograveur*, built in 1959, Tinguely made a precarious-looking device from welded lengths of scrap metal with an elevated seat and pedals; pushing on the pedals drives an elaborate system of differently sized wheels that causes a felt pen to draw circles on a sheet of paper, the position of which can be adjusted. (The impression of the whole is not dissimilar to a large, unruly Spirograph, the invention of which *Cyclograveur* preceded by half a decade.)

Tinguely's work was made in reaction to the postwar boom in consumption and mass production, particularly in the United States. In this era of increasingly mechanized industrial processes, he foresaw, with uncanny prescience, a society in which man would be beholden to machines – a situation he described as 'real madness'. Foregrounding automation and chance, his constructions deny conventional assumptions about art as the product of individual genius, but they are equally wary of machines. One of his most famous pieces, *Homage to New York*, was a towering assembly of eighty bicycle wheels, glass bottles, saws, an old piano and a baby's pram, among other things, which (intentionally) self-destructed over the course of half an hour in the same garden at the Museum of Modern Art into which *Bicycle Wheel* had been thrown some thirty-five years later.

LUCY AND JORGE ORTA

Cloud – MIU Tricycle, 2012–14

Lucy Orta was working in *haute couture* in Paris when she met her future husband, the artist Jorge Orta, in 1991. At that time, the French economy, like much of the world, was suffering in the wake of the 1987 stock-market crash and the Gulf War. Her first pieces were portable shelters that transformed into items of clothing – a response to the influx of refugees fleeing the Gulf conflict, and the rising numbers of homeless people she encountered in the streets of Paris.

Always containing a practical proposal, or provocation, the Ortas' work responds to crises – be these social, economic or environmental. Since 2005, one of their primary focuses has been water scarcity: water as a basic right and necessity for survival, but also as an industry; a commodity to be packaged, marketed, bought and sold. Inspired by the bundles of empty plastic bottles gathered by the *Zabbaleen* ('garbage people') communities in Cairo, who sort nearly two-thirds of the city's waste in an informal system of collection and exchange, the Ortas' 'Cloud' works (2010–ongoing) conjoin empty water bottles through layers of papier-mâché, which are covered with resin and then painted shimmering metallic blue. Recalling both clouds and lakes, these lumpen forms physicalize the two different systems in which water circulates: the natural and the industrial. In one sculpture, *Cloud – MIU Tricycle* (2012–14), a towering blue cloud sits in the back of a customized cargo trike – a reminder, perhaps, of the *Zabbaleen*'s improvised system of waste collection, as well as an emblem of the clean technologies and small scales of production that will be crucial if we are to avert environmental disaster.

OVER HERE AND
OVER THERE

David Millar and Guy Andrews
Photographs by Bernard Thompson
and Taz Darling

FAUSTO COPPI
Live at the Royal Albert Hall

The great Italian *Campionissimo*, Fausto Coppi, was billed as 'the greatest roadman and pursuit rider of the day' when he was flown over from Italy to London to appear at the Royal Albert Hall for *Cycling Magazine*'s Diamond Jubilee celebration in 1951. This grand showcase of traditional British entertainment was presented to an audience of club cyclists, combining a mixture of roller racing and cabaret acts on the stage – quite frankly, it must have been bewildering to Coppi and his entourage. Here was a man who had won the Giro d'Italia, the Tour de France and Paris–Roubaix, and he was being billed alongside a group of amateur racers and circus performers.

This bizarre variety evening featured comedy acrobats, the Chevalier Brothers, Bobby Howell and his Orchestra and an Australian juggler among many other novelty turns. It must have been a strange night to say the least, especially when Coppi was presented to the capacity audience of 5,000 riding his bike atop a pair of warm-up rollers on a spotlit stage, something that must have seemed a little like a circus sideshow. Coppi was then asked questions put forward by the crowd via his French friend and fellow rider, Jean Bobet (brother of Louison, the Tour de France winner), who also spoke English and Italian.

Whatever he said probably lost a lot in translation.

Over There [opposite]: Fausto Coppi had film-star looks, and class on the bike to match. He won the Giro d'Italia five times and the Tour de France twice, and several one-day classics and championships too. His winning ways gave him the nickname *il Campionissimo* – the champion of champions.

Over Here: Bernard Thompson, renowned British photographer of the 1960s to 1980s, photographed some of the greatest British riders of the 20th century, including Beryl Burton (pictured here), Alf Engers and Tommy Simpson.

BRITISH SPORT HAS ALWAYS BEEN REGARDED AS A LITTLE ODD. While the British invented a great variety of games and sports, they made the mistake of exporting them around the world, where other cultures made them their own and set about perfecting them. Football, cricket and rugby were all born in the British Isles, and are all now played wonderfully in the Southern Hemisphere, far away from the fields in which they were first devised – and no doubt in far better weather. British sport wasn't about winning so much as it was about the rules, all generated by men in blazers and debated for hours in smoke-filled committee rooms and gentlemen's clubs – the British organized sports well, while foreign countries simply concentrated on playing them.

The first officially recorded bike race happened in Paris, France, in 1868, and it was won by an Englishman, James Moore. Despite Moore's winning start, British cycle sport had a turbulent history. For the next 150 years, as continental cyclists realized that racing together in a bunch was a great idea, the British concluded that it was much more sporting to race alone. Time trialling was regarded as the way to do it. By the turn of the 20th century, all forms of cycle racing had been banned on the UK's open roads by the National Cyclists' Union (NCU) because of fears of 'dangerous riding', and races could only be held on velodromes and closed circuits. This was, in part, the result of several political splits in cycling's governing bodies that set the tone for the next century of cycle sport in Britain, and it was a categorical disaster for the sport. Police would stop the now-illegal road races and charge groups of 'lunatic cyclists' on horseback, so cycle racing was forced underground.

Time trials became popular because you rode alone and could pretend you weren't racing. Secret locations and early starts also meant that these races could be done without the police knowing. The roads used for these events were given code names, so clubs could promote events and competitors would know where to go; these codes are still used today. Time trialling has a reputation for being boring, and is hardly a spectator sport, but the reality is that at its outset in the UK it was perfect for a belligerent group of cyclists just wanting to carry on competing. In the early part of the 20th century they even wore black jackets and plus fours, an outfit known as an

Alpaca, after the wool it was made from. They wore this so as to be inconspicuous; if they were stopped by the police they would lie and never let on that there was a race happening. They looked like office workers who were late for a meeting, and in the summer heat this heavy woollen costume became unbearable.

Eventually the law relaxed, but it was only in the post-war period that road racing began to gain popularity. Before then, in 1933, the Union Cycliste Internationale (UCI) had already begun road racing at World Championships, but Britain lagged behind; in 1942 Percy Stallard organized a renegade race on the open road, known as a 'massed start', and he was immediately banned by the NCU. Stallard then formed the British League of Racing Cyclists and the two organizations fought each other bitterly, until they merged in 1959 to form the British Cycling Federation. There's no doubt that the years of turmoil and legal battles held cycling back as a sport in the UK, yet despite the uncertainties and squabbling, it was the cyclists who found a way of competing and refused to back down.

The result of banning riding in bunches on the road meant cycling lived out much of the 20th century as a mostly amateur sport with only a small professional circuit. British pros were nothing compared to those in France, Italy, Belgium or Spain. This meant very few riders travelled abroad, and when they did, they experienced quite a culture shock, because continental European cycling and British cycling were polar opposites. It seems British cycling has only really caught up to the rest of the world in the last ten years.

Over Here: Hardly the most exciting spectator sport; British children watch the classic time trial racing scene, 1960s.

Over Here [top]: The start of a time trial. A rider gets a decent shove from the 'pusher off' as the timekeeper counts down his start time: 5, 4, 3, 2, 1, Go! In France the time trial is known as *contre la montre* ('against the clock'), and it is known by racers everywhere as the 'Race of Truth'.

Over Here [bottom left]: The 'dead turn' is a very British time-trial peculiarity. To ensure that the distance was exact, a marshall would stand in the road to signal the point at which a rider would need to make a U-turn and retrace his path to the finish.

Over Here [bottom right]: The lone rider sweeps through a sleepy British village; milk bottles and newspapers await breakfast time. Time trials always mean an early start, sometimes before anyone is up and about.

Over There [overleaf]: Tour de France 1960, stage 17 from Briaçon to Aix Les Bains. The Italian Gastone Nencini won the stage and the Tour outright. The Tour de France always travels through some incredible French scenery. It was established to promote the newspaper *l'Auto*, although it also managed to successfully promote the French countryside to a wider audience.

Over There: David Millar,
photographed in Biarritz, 2016.

Over Here [overleaf]: A bewildered
couple outside their house in
Yorkshire watch as the 2008 British
National Championships road race
peloton speeds past.

STRAIGHT FROM
THE HORSE'S MOUTH

We talk to ex-professional rider David Millar
about his experiences in the peloton. As a British
road and time trial champion, and an eleven-time
Tour de France finisher, among other things, he knows
all about the differences between racing
'Over Here' and 'Over There'.

I WAS PRO BY THE TIME I WAS NINETEEN. I did a few time trials in the UK, but during my summer holidays I went to Belgium. The British racers were saying 'you're too young to go road racing', but there were too many rules, they didn't understand it. I was lucky as I had no [cycling] heritage and I loved road racing. I really saw it as two different sports: the British version and the continental one. Road racing in Britain would be like someone playing cricket in France. But over there, they understand it, and I fell in love with the sport not because of what it could bring me, but because of what it was and what it is.

The biggest thing I learned about British bike racing was that you couldn't ever give up. Eventually everyone's gonna get tired. After 100 kilometres of following and chasing everything at a National Championship race, inevitably everyone would soon be buggered. I hated racing the British scene because it was just so hard. Always a negative race. They were really good, motivated bike riders – and it was a different style of racing, so you were dealing with an onslaught – but I used to lose my cool. 'Ah fuck it! I can't beat all of you!' Several generations of British riders could have been excellent continental pros. They had opportunities but they saw the continental scene as… well, they just didn't get it. It was a different game, it wasn't just the usual British slog-fest. British riders are well-respected these days and

have been for a while, recognized and admired for their tough, never-say-die attitude… this stems from a racing culture in Britain that celebrates the 'last man standing' – where the race starts out on the rivet and stays there until somebody prevails.

Road racing had been untouched in the UK for the last 75 years, but that means it's old-fashioned, 'pure' road racing. It's been equally hard for continental riders to understand time trials [as it has been for us to understand road racing]. The French always looked down on time trialling. Worst-case scenario, it's a day off, or a pain in the arse. Never a cool discipline, but it wasn't always like that. Cyrille Guimard was my first professional director, and when I was nineteen, he had a vision. Even as a neo pro, getting my head kicked in, he came into my room after a time trial and he said to me, 'David, you must always ride every single time trial *à bloc*'. That was how he operated and he instilled that drive in his riders. Most of the French wouldn't take this advice, but when it came to marginal gains, Guimard was Sky before Sky.

It was always the soigneurs. That's where all the knowledge came from, not the other riders or your *directeur sportif* (DS). The soigneurs would tell you off because they ran the ship: 'Why are you on your feet? Standing in the corridor? I'll bring it to you. Go lie down.' You're mildly brainwashed to think about nothing

but the bike race. It was very hard to argue with their old wives' tales – 'air con is bad', 'you can't have the window down!' – all these. It seemed that wearing scarves if you're sick, not eating certain things, taking the middle bit out of baguettes… you have to do it because they knew more about it than we did. Soigneur is a very appropriate word for them, to 'take care' and 'look after'.

They also instilled the culture in us; they had a middle management role, if you like. They were your shoulders to cry on. They were weird dudes. Soigneurs came with you as part of the package. That doesn't happen anymore, but it gave them status too – you moved together. The soigneurs kept the gentlemen's rules better than the gentlemen. They were our base of knowledge – we didn't share anything with each other. They passed on the knowledge. Perhaps that was the ultimate secret society. No one knew what hold they had on the riders. Old soigneurs' tales rather than old wives' tales. Even the DS learned things from soigneurs. But that's changed now.

And then there was the language; at the time, we had none of the sport's culture. Even if Greg LeMond had been the first English-speaking winner of the Tour de France, he was basically a Francophile. Chris Boardman was just a British bike rider who was an amazing cyclist, he didn't learn the language, nor was he a road racer. There was no history of 'us' being road racers, and the lingua franca at the time was French. We barely learned the language; you knew what the words meant in terms of racing [but nothing deeper than that]. We learnt *peloton*, *échappé*, and so on, but we didn't know the etymologies. But you get respect

if you learn the language. I didn't speak any French at first but I knew that if I wanted to turn pro I had to go to France or Belgium. (Spain didn't really figure on my radar, and neither did Italy – I think it's because both were just further away.) When I got there, it was a sport that was basically completely different to the British version.

Only shit riders swore. Only the loudmouths. Then they got a label and it was a sign of weakness – because real pros didn't need to swear. I remember Lance Armstrong – we got on very well – in his interviews, the respect he showed for all the stars, but then we were in the peloton, and he was like 'who the fuck does he think he is?' He thrived on hate; he had to hate his opponents, he had to have zero respect, which was a really weird thing. That was his energy. On the other hand, Miguel Indurain didn't have a gram of hate in him, yet he was a fierce competitor. Spanish guys don't use hate in races, they're very humble racers. They don't mind showing weakness but they can still smash it at the end. Whereas American riders are like, 'I'm fine, man, so that was easy.' Americans had a common culture, an outsider/rebel [approach], because they were the new kids on the block. But one thing that Lance brought was [the fact that] he didn't give a shit about European culture. He was your stereotypical comic-book American; brash. And behind closed doors, he was like, 'who the fuck do these people think they are? Fuck 'em!' A lot of guys think they can bring this hate, some shout a lot, mostly because they're highly stressed. Europeans don't do that as much in the peloton. Lance didn't stop after the race though, he continued. Lance would hate you in and out of the race. The Americans feel

Over Here: 'I can't beat you all!' David Millar (left, removing sunglasses) with exhausted British-based professional riders at the finish of the 2008 British National Road Race, a race that has always been won by the 'last man standing'.

they have to be dominant, aggressive to fit in. It's not the British way… but, who knows, maybe that's why the Americans found it easier to fit in?

In my day, the neo pros were all on the same salary. It was as much conditioning as anything else, to ask the question, 'do you have the character?' – the neo pro way is to be treated like a bitch for two years [new or first-year professionals are always *domestiques* first]. Every race you have no programme, no options; you become cultural survivalists. Then you become a team player. Ultimately you don't pass any information on from these days because you 'fuckin' did it the hard way and you can't complain because that shows weakness of character'. You had to go through the system. It was like a queue, a pecking order. A lot of top British riders were essentially homeboys, but I had a healthy detachment due to my ex-pat upbringing. The reason we don't have a riders' union as such is because we're not union people – we're mercenaries. The paradox is, it's a team sport, but you reach the top level because you're a loner. A genetic freak. That's the origin. At Junior level, you move through the ranks so quickly… then you turn pro, it's been your dream the whole time but all of a sudden you're just a tiny cog. In order to survive, you have to be quiet and fuckin' take it.

Over There [top]: Francesco Moser, the classic Italian professional who had style on and off the bike. Like Fausto Coppi, he became a legend with the Italian fans, the group of supporters known in Italy as the *tifosi*.

Over There [below]: Phil Anderson at the 1982 Tour de France. One of the first English-speaking riders to do very well as a professional, and the first Australian to wear the coveted Yellow Jersey.

It's a completely different sport now to Merckx's era. Things were different back in the day. We've got quite a snobbery in our sport, you have to learn the hard way. It became almost nascent, as you were earning your stripes. I got into the sport in 1992 when I was fifteen. At that point, it was Indurain. I started to watch the races and he was such a silent person, he bossed the race without any threats. I was watching one of the Spanish races and there was some attacking down the front, and some faux pas was going on; Indurain came along and he simply put his hand on the back of the rider who was causing all the trouble, and you sensed this power. He didn't need to do any shouting or bullying. It was a contrast to Bernard Hinault, who led with an iron fist, literally. And Eddy Merckx, who led through fear and domination, and Lance Armstrong, too, which then turned into something totally different.

Football teams are often judged by their style of play. If a new manager shuts all that down, the fans are in uproar. The fans would rather lose in glory than play in shame. People embrace the risk of failure, which is why people love cycling. Alberto Contador is amazing. The dude is the best grand tour bike racer of his generation. If he's in second, third, place   he's never satisfied. He'd rather finish 11th than 2nd. It means so much

to him but he's not afraid of failure – this is the paradox. That culture is not lost – 'I don't care if we finish 2nd, or 5th, or 6th' – let's just rip this race to pieces. Other riders have always helped him but that wasn't money – that was respect. That's why bike racing is such a good sport, that's why it's lasted so long and been through so much shit.

After the finish line, you won't shout, you're zoned out, there's no emotion. A lot of the guys never talk about bad shit, never get worked up. In the team bus after a race, you joke about it. The general rule is that if you've got that far in the sport, you don't like putting your head above the parapet. Make sure everything is cool. But you *never* make enemies as a pro; you learn that if you want to make it, and survive within the peloton, you can't make enemies.

Brian Robinson was one of the first riders to go to the continent and do rather well. I didn't know of Brian or many of the other British ex-pros at the time I started out. But then again, I didn't know that much. As a teenager, I was into the modern era, so it was only after years of learning that I found I had more in common with the Aussies than the British. It was like the foreign legion still existed. The oeuvre of bike-racing literature in Britain was minimal in the nineties too…

In my first season, we ended up being the best amateur team in France that year. I could see there were a number of guys who could be pro, but weren't pro, and I learned later that there was a lot of drugs going on in the team. But I was being protected and taken under different wings; you could see the hierarchies and how the personalities all operated together. There was a massive underworld scene – and that was just the amateur teams in France. I survived the first two years through complete naivety, not knowing what to look for; some riders protect you while other riders would use you.

I saw myself as a European and I was very much part of the old-school peloton, where we were all on such short-term contracts we never had the prospect of joining any long-term teams that had your best interests in mind. We were very mercurial. The peloton is organic, you have to survive to get into it and the teams had to rotate, but that kind of group you had as a peloton, you had to figure out ways of working together and not picking fights. I enjoyed the fact that racing was slightly deviant and weird, and mostly that it was a big game. Back in those days, you were forming little mafias, making deals and so on… But the guys were clever, it was all shifty. We didn't socialize; you finish the race, you wouldn't see another bike racer until the next one. No ties whatsoever. The only tie we had was the unity we had when we were together, on the road.

Over Here: A racing cyclist with nowhere to hide – the early-morning loneliness of the British time trial.

Le Rosbif [lə ʁɔsbif]

à bloc [a blɔk]

tout à droite [tu a dʁwa]

'ON THE RIVET' – THE CLASSIC ENGLISH CYCLING TERM for being at the limit of your speed. Language in cycle racing is very important, especially when describing suffering. Over here the etymology is a bit outdated these days, as modern plastic-covered racing saddles no longer have the copper-topped rivets that hold the leather hide to the frame of the saddle underneath. It made sense because as riders crouch further forward over the handlebars to place more power into the pedals, they naturally end up right on the tip of the saddle where the rivet would have been, hence 'on the rivet' – Brooks's trademark feature.

In Italian, they'd say **al gancio**, which means 'on the hook' – like meat in an abattoir – just like on the rivet, you're right on the limit and if the pace picks up even a tiny bit you'll be **cotto**; 'cooked'. It's a similar expression in Spanish, although **el gancho** has a slightly different connotation, of being 'on the hook' like a fish, the action fitting with gasping for air and leaning forward like a fish being pulled from the water. Also, Italians wouldn't simply say 'full gas' when referring to big efforts; instead they'll use **al cento per cento**. 100%.

And when Cyrille Guimard told David to ride **à bloc** (at block), he was using the preferred French term for their all-out efforts. Sometimes French racers will say **tout à droite**, or 'everything to the right', referring to the position of the chain on the sprockets. To a French cyclist **Le Rosbif** – slang for 'rôti de bœuf', or 'roast beef' – has always been the unflattering nickname for most British riders, and a team or group of them would often be referred to as **Les Rosbifs**.

Aside from the nicknames, there are words that define a rider's skills and place in the team's hierarchy. And the names for support riders are equally unflattering. The French call them **domestiques**, although many prefer the Italian **gregario** which seems less demeaning than simply someone who does the laundry. **Gregario** is an old Roman term for foot soldier, and has a familiar air of camaraderie. **Domestique** can be either insulting or complimentary depending on who you ask, although a **domestique deluxe** is not simply a bottle boy, it's a bottle boy who can also race a bike. The Flemish, Belgians and Dutch would call domestiques **knecht**, which is as demeaning as it sounds – it means, simply, servant. Once their apprenticeship of pain and suffering is done, you become what the French call a **coureur**, literally a 'runner', but it can also be complimentary, as you might say in English, to be a 'bit of a hitter' – it sets a rider apart from a mere **cycliste** (amateur leisure rider) or a simple **équipier** (team rider).

Then you'll be categorized further, into the type of racer you are. These are harder to define in different languages but, as ever, the French lead the way. Perhaps best of all is their swashbuckling **baroudeur**, the perfect definition for an attacking rider who has all the hallmarks of a musketeer, a rider who never says die. A rider with the legs to kick at the end of a hard stage and who has the high-speed cruising ability to stay clear of the best lead-out teams. The **baroudeur**'s favourite move is the **coup de chacal**, or 'jackal's trick', what we know as the last-minute escape, usually delivered when a breakaway has just been caught and often in the last kilometre of the race; effective attacks need to be super fast and have the element of surprise. Invariably it ends in failure, which is why we love a **baroudeur** all the more when it pans out.

a bagnomaria [a baɲɲomarja]

chasse patate [ʃas patat]

The **rouleur** is a roadman-sprinter type who can still win a race but is usually regarded as a time trial or classics specialist rather than a Tour de France podium contender – **rouleurs** are often the great team captains, like Gilbert Duclos-Lassalle or our own David Millar, and they can also be the great classics winners, like Sean Kelly or Francesco Moser. Not all fit the mould though; five-time Tour de France winner Eddy Merckx was a thoroughbred **rouleur**, perhaps the greatest the sport has ever seen, and he could climb alright too.

A **puncheur** is a rider suited to those hilly days when you need to be both climber and road racer – needless to say the French love a **puncheur** – brave with a hint of **panache** (flamboyant class or style). A **grimpeur** is a pure climber, and in English what we'd refer to as 'honking' when riding up a hill – which mostly sounds like you're making animal noises, struggling and wheezing – is in French known as riding **en danseuse**, 'dancing on the pedals' – standing on the pedals out of the saddle. Beautifully poetic.

When British professional riders are wheeled out at awards evenings and celebrations these days Brian Robinson is never too far from the spotlight. Brian was one of the few that made it, simply stating that 'I just went over there and did what they did'. To this day Robinson is remembered fondly in the French media as a **puncheur** who had style and grace on the bike and was always polite and courteous off it. He 'got it' and set about his work in a pragmatic and no-nonsense way and, no matter where in the world you are, that is what bike racing is all about.

In Italian the best slang is about the riders' behaviour, so they have a **succhiaruote**, a 'wheel sucker', and their version of a pace-setting **rouleur** is the brutish-sounding **battistrada** – quite literally a 'road beater'. Italians would use **passista** for someone who was more tactically aware, like a team captain. Their expressions are subtle, often with hidden meaning; for example, a **gregario** could be sent to **tirare il collo**, that is, up the pace a bit; not enough to break away but enough to put your rivals in difficulty and wear them down. Tactical sporting nous is something the Italians know all about; they win at all costs and, as in football, the rules of racing are more complex in Italy.

Tired riders dropped from the breakaway may then find themselves caught out on the road on their own, or bridging across to the break. Either way they're in 'no man's land', a place nobody wants to be stuck for long, no matter where they come from. The Italians call this being **a bagnomaria**, or 'in a double-boiler', a bowl over a boiling pan of water used in cooking – always thinking about food, those Italians. The French term is slightly odd too, because **chasse patate** is literally the 'potato chase'. It apparently derives from six-day track racing, where post-meal races (that invariably included lots of potatoes) often involved attempts to break away after dinner that seemed doomed to failure, when the riders all had bellies full of starchy carbs – a potato can, however, also be used in French slang to denote an idiot, which sounds like a far more likely origin.

Making it into the breakaway but not intending to work the British would call 'sitting in', or 'sitting on', usually done to protect a team mate or leader in the peloton behind. In some cases it's just to save energy to attack or out-sprint your breakaway companions. This rider is never very

al cento per cento [al tʃento per tʃento]

popular in the breakaway and is often referred to as the 'ticket collector'. Not to be confused with another railway-influenced term, **lanterne rouge**, after the red lantern that hangs on the back of a train and in cycling celebrates the last rider in a stage race like the Tour de France. It's quite an honour being last at the world's biggest bike race, and believe it or not it's something that demands considerable respect.

Speaking the language of cycling certainly helps you understand what's going on around you, and the more experienced the riders, regardless of whether they finish first or last, the more respect they seem to have for the history and terminology of their trade. No matter where the words came from, the language of racing has always been universal. Being 'taken out the back' is the sly tactic of missing a turn in order to create a gap that must be closed; the result can be that the 'gapped' rider cannot manage to close it, enabling the other rider to attack from behind and drop them. In Italian you might say **fare il buco**, 'make the hole', when you're in a group and you drop off the back, either because you're cooked or you're thinking tactically – it just refers to the hole or gap you leave in front of you. It's a heartless tactic and is used by non-sprinters as a defence, usually before the finish or a hard part of the race course, like a hill. Then you are **lâché** or **largé**, which simply means being dropped from the group.

In a sprint, to **fermer la porte** would involve some strong-arm tactics, as 'shutting the door' on an opponent means riding into a space that another is intending to ride into, the rules being that if you are in front you have right of way, sort of. Lead-outs and sprinting in professional bike races are fast and furious, and there's not much room for explanation; if a rider moves off their line and blocks another rider, it can be regarded as either a smart move or dangerous riding, depending on your point of view.

The Italian **gruppetto** is the universal term for the group of dropped riders that gang together on the final climbs of a big mountain stage, what we British would call the 'laughing group' and the French **l'autobus**, although those guys are hardly slow and heavy like a bus (and they are rarely laughing either).

At the other end of the race, it's the **testa della corsa** in Italian rather than the clunky-sounding English 'head of the race'; the French call it **tête de la course**, while **cabeza de la raza** in Spanish certainly sounds like a race… And the fact that what we would call 'the bunch', the French call the **peloton** and Italians call a **gruppo** – also their name for the group of parts you equip your bike with – well, it all just sounds right.

The Italians don't seem to have a definitive term for a breakaway; their usual term, **la fuga**, means flight, which is descriptive enough. Back in France, an **échappée** translates as an escape, what we would call a breakaway, and a **bidon** is your water bottle. A 'water-bottle escape' doesn't really make sense, but an **échappée bidon** is what the French would call an early or soft breakaway. This was usually a set-up for lowly riders or teams to get some TV airtime. Sometimes there is a tactical reason, or it could simply be that a local rider allowed some space so that their family could see them at the head of the field, just for a while.

el gancho [el gantʃo]

al gancio [al gantʃo]

As the peloton starts to reel in a breakaway, a tired rider might **faire l'élastique**, literally 'do the elastic'; in English we'd say 'breaking the elastic' or 'swinging off the back', but either way this is used as a term for resilience, clawing back onto the group as the gap widens. At this point a rider might have to take a **bidon au miel** from the team car, literally 'a bottle of honey' or what we'd call 'a sticky bottle', where a rider would hang from the vehicle to get a tow, pretending they are taking a drink.

Climbers fear the wind more than most. Alongside the cobbles of Flanders and Northern France, windy days are best dealt with by the **Flahutes** (Flemish tough guys), strongmen on the flat, who can strike fear into the hearts of the sub-60 kilometre **grimpeurs**. The wind brings danger to General Classification (GC) contenders, who will use tough tactics to distance a rival too – ever wondered why a team leader always has at least one ever-present team chaperone? It's to stop them being bullied by the big boys – GC contenders live in constant fear of being left behind, and the possibility of being caught in **un coup de bordure**, literally, 'a stab in the gutter'. It's a rare but effective tactic to create diagonal lines of riders that form in a cross-winds. If there's only enough room for ten riders across the road, then that is how many will form the **échelon**, which translates as a 'rung' in a ladder, but refers to the formation, which resembles a line of migrating geese. Another **échelon** can form directly behind this one, but as the wind blows the gaps can quickly grow and put the lead echelon further ahead. In English we might say that a rider has been 'guttered' – that is, squeezed out of the **échelon** and not allowed to take shelter. Not to be confused with when the race is at full stretch and the peloton is 'lined out' in a single string of riders wheel to wheel – the usual sign that things are very fast indeed.

While the French, Italians, Spanish and Belgians have hundreds of terms that only get used in cycling, there are fewer phrases and words in English that mean very little outside the world of cycle racing, but still work so well. For example, 'glass cranking' can refer to two types of riding: either taking it easy on your turn in a breakaway because you are saving something for later, or riding slowly because you're simply spent. Then there's 'pedalling squares', and we all know how that feels, the result of 'blowing up' or 'bonking', or 'getting the knock'… what the Italians, rather unimaginatively, call a **crisi di fame** or 'hunger crisis'.

Cycle sport's unique appeal is that racing is still a journey, as much as any adventure, you just don't get much of a chance to look at the view and stop for a coffee. Experienced professional racers become hardened travellers, what were once referred to as **les Forçats de la Route** – the Convicts of the Road – their life has always been one that is constantly on the move. Over here, the English language doesn't create the same historical romance of the French or literary meaning of the Italians; 'meeting the man with the hammer' is as poetic as it gets when it comes to describing running out of energy, when it's time to **avoir tout à gauche** – make sure you have 'everything to the left', as they'd say over there.

BORN IN BRUM

Photographs by Martin Parr

'I don't like being flattered. It doesn't suit my English sensibilities. Remember, we are the great country of understatement.'
Martin Parr

Despite this sentiment, and like it or not, Martin Parr is one of Britain's best-known photographers, whose work often explores Britain's towns and cities, purposely pursuing the idea of what it means to be British. In the autumn of 2015 he travelled to the Brooks Factory in Smethwick, one of the last remaining manufacturers in the industrial West Midlands, a place once known as the engine room of British manufacturing and an area that was also at the centre of the world's bicycle industry for almost a century. Here, Martin portrays the Brooks people and the workshop from which the iconic leather saddle still comes into the world, from the place that's always been known as the Black Country, in the heart of Britain.

In order of appearance:

MICHAEL BELL .... BLANKING PRESS OPERATOR

PHILIP WEBB .... SADDLE-FRAME WELDER

GURDIP KAUR .... PRESS OPERATOR

STEPHEN BELL .... LEADER OF THE FRAME ASSEMBLY DEPARTMENT

JAYNE HOGAN .... PRESS OPERATOR

DIANE CLAY .... LEADER OF THE LEATHER FINISHING DEPARTMENT

RIKKI RAVENHILL .... LEATHER 'CLICKING PRESS' OPERATOR

LUCASZ KUSLIK .... LEATHER PREPARATION DEPARTMENT

ERIC MURRAY AND JOHN POPE .... SOLID RIVETTERS

JOLANTA JONES .... FINAL ASSEMBLY AND PACKING

ANTHONY CROSDALE .... SOLID RIVETTER

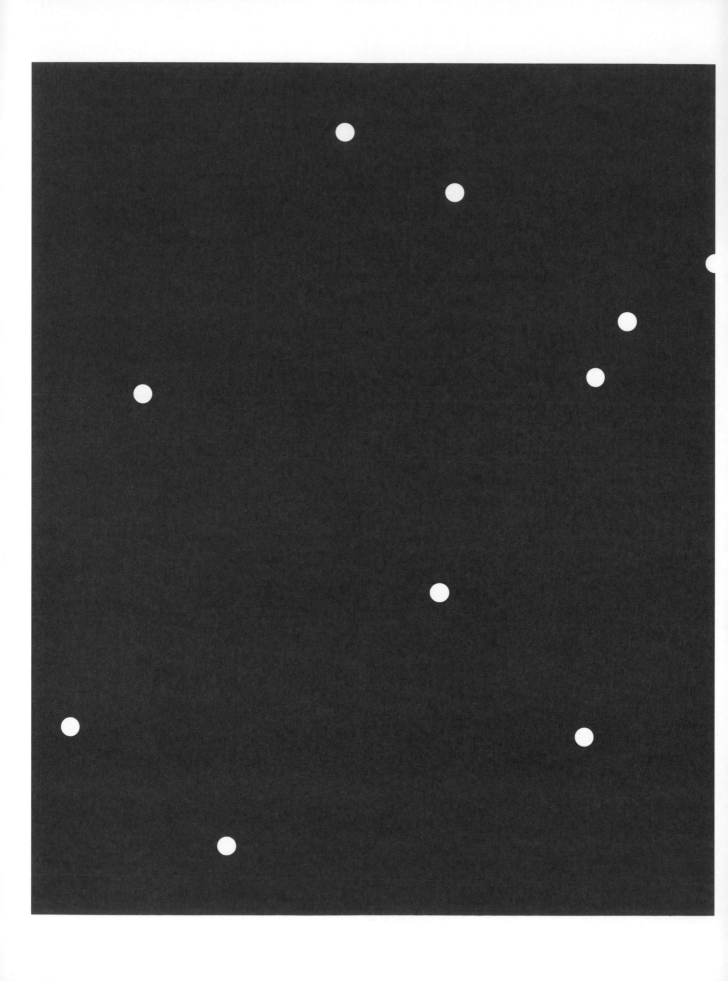

PILGRIMS AND PIONEERS

Jack Thurston
Illustrations by Laura Quick

LINES IN THE LANDSCAPE

Every little vista, every little glimpse that we have of what lies before us, gives the impatient imagination rein, so that it can outstrip the body and already plunge into the shadow of the woods, and overlook from the hilltop the plain beyond it, and wander in the windings of the valleys that are still far in front. The road is already there – we shall not be long behind.
Robert Louis Stevenson

Robert Louis Stevenson was among the first modern writers to turn his travels into great literature, whether sailing on the high seas, tramping along on foot or walking with a donkey across the French Cévennès. Stevenson died in 1894, just at the beginning of the great bicycle boom, and there is no record of him ever having ridden a bike. Yet he loved roads, and he would surely have taken quite naturally to riding them by bicycle. Stevenson knew well the 'sympathy of mood' that develops between the traveller and the road and how the road itself becomes a companion on a long journey. He saw roads, with their 'lithe contortions' and 'capricious sinuosities', as objects of beauty.

Roads, tracks, paths and trails were the first marks that *Homo sapiens* made on the face of the planet. Of course the very earliest weren't made by people at all, but by vast herds of migrating animals. Our nomadic hunter-gatherer ancestors merely followed along behind with their stomachs rumbling. Ever since, the idea of the open road has always been a powerful one: a chance to wipe the slate clean and embrace a future of unlimited possibility. As Jack Kerouac put it in *On the Road*: 'Nothing behind me, everything ahead of me, as is ever so on the road'.

To travel the open road is – by definition – to follow in the footsteps, or tyre-tracks, of multitudes who have gone before. For the racing cyclist, a climb of the great mountain roads of the Alps and Pyrenees may bring to mind a celebrated rider who rode to glory on those very slopes. The imagination of the touring cyclist casts a wider net, and our rides retrace the journeys of more ancient wayfarers, from Celtic traders and wandering bards to Roman legionaries, pilgrims, drovers, tinkers, vagabonds and migrants.

Yet for much of human history, overland travel was painfully slow and fraught with danger. Roads could be dire: impassably rocky, overgrown or thick with mud. Bandits and highwaymen preyed on the defenceless. The word 'travel' comes from the Old French *travail*, to labour or to toil. Canals and railways promised new, easier ways of travelling, and for a time roads fell into decline. The rebirth of roads for long-distance travel owes a huge debt to the bicycle, and to the desire of pioneering cyclists to escape noisy, soot-blackened towns and cities for a prelapsarian countryside idyll, 'roving', as the French novelist Émile Zola put it, 'along a thousand freely chosen paths'.

People fell in love with the bicycle, the quintessential product of the machine age, because it gave them a way to leave the industrial world behind. The romance of the open road is as powerful as it's ever been.

A Roman Legionary

"Blonde Wendy law, and Brunette Shirley Duncan"

- movie tone News, - Video footage, 1946, Australia.

FREEDOM

In 1901, Henry Spickler of Polo, Illinois, set out to travel around the world by bicycle, without a cent in his pocket. Up until then, long-distance cyclists had either been independently wealthy or were sponsored by travel magazines and bicycle manufacturers. When the 1890s bike boom went bust, the sponsors disappeared and the era of the hobo cyclist began. Spickler's account of his three-year, forty-thousand-mile journey contains a complete list of the jobs that he took on along the way:

> Acrobat, advertiser, agent, auto-mechanic, athletics, bank collector, barber, bell-hop, bill-poster, buyer, card-letterer, carpenter, cashier, cattleman, companion, cook, correspondent, demonstrator, devil, ditcher, driver, editorial writer, entertainer, eye-doctor, farmer, food-collector, foreman, fruit-picker, gardener, grinder, guard, guide, gymnast, hairdresser, hat-cleaner, hired-man, hotel runner, ice cream maker, interpreter, jam maker, janitor, juggler, labourer, lecturer, lodge organizer, magnetic healer, manager, masseur, messenger-boy, monologist, packer, painter, palmist, peddler, pen artist, photographer, poet, preacher, publisher, railroader, roustabout, sailor, salesman, signature-writer, singer, sleight-of-hand, solicitor, stamp-collector, stenographer, stevedore, teacher, trick cyclist, waiter, window dresser and wood-chopper.

In the same year a Japanese adventurer, Harukichi Nakamura, set off on his own 'dead broke' tour of the world, earning his way, like Spickler, by taking on a dazzling variety of odd jobs. Wendy Law Suart and Shirley Duncan spent three years travelling the length and breadth of 1940s Australia, and were the first women to cycle the vast, desolate Nullarbor Plain. They earned their way cattle ranching, selling sandwiches, and working in a canning factory. In 1952, Abbott Dugally left home in Los Angeles with $8 in his pocket and returned ten years later with $12. He earned his way playing the harmonica, performing acrobatic stunts and begging donations: a self-styled bicycling vagabond. 'Some people think I'm crazy,' he said, 'others envy me.' Today, most people who set out on a big bicycle adventure first save up a pot of money and once on the road try to eke it out for as long as possible. This sets an inevitable point at which the adventure must end: when the cash runs out. Earning money along the way elevates the bicycle traveller into a true nomad. The greatest cycling vagabond of them all is Heinz Stücke. In 1962, aged twenty-two, he set out from his home town in the German Rhineland and remained on the road for half a century, circling the globe six times. He supported himself by selling postcards and pamphlets about his travels to people he met along the way.

Taking the age-old tradition of working your passage and applying it to a bicycle adventure is to reject the bicycle tour as a bourgeois leisure pursuit, an extended holiday to be followed by a return to 'real life'. This makes a bicycle tour a little less like the old Grand Tours of the British nobility and a little more like the original 'Tour de France', which was an essential rite of passage undertaken by French apprentice craftsmen. With modern-day restrictions on work permits, it is unlikely that any self-sustaining bicycle traveller could match Henry Spickler for sheer variety of employment, but any cyclist who decides to work their way around the world can expect to find their journey every bit as satisfying.

SPEED

As soon as people realized it was possible to get from here to there on a bicycle, thoughts turned to how fast… Early tests of bicycling speed were held on racecourses, with wood and iron velocipedes taking the place of horses and riders standing in for jockeys. It wasn't long before people were wondering how a cyclist might fare on longer, place-to-place journeys. In 1868, Albert Laumaillé wrote to Pierre Micheaux, whose factory made the first velocipedes, asking for a special machine 'of the greatest solidity, capable of supporting the longest journeys without breaking down', and he used it for a summer tour of Brittany. Seven years later, on a British-built high wheeler, Laumaillé raced a rider on horseback over the seven hundred miles from Paris to Vienna. He won by three days. In 1882 Ion Keith-Falconer, one of the fastest bike racers of his generation, rode from Land's End to John o' Groats in thirteen days, following a circuitous route of more than a thousand miles.

Even as bicycle racing evolved into a codified sport of its own, solo, long-distance place-to-place rides retained a popular romantic appeal. They were also perfect publicity stunts for bicycle manufacturers to demonstrate the speed and reliability of their products. Charles Terront was France's first cycling superstar and may also claim the title of the world's first ultra-endurance bike racer. In 1891 he won the first Paris–Brest–Paris race. At 743 miles it was more than twice the distance of any previous road race. Terront rode a British Humber bicycle fitted with Michelin's prototype inflatable tyres. He followed this up in 1893 by riding from St Petersburg to Paris, covering nearly two thousand miles in fourteen days. His support team followed from town to town by train. The next year, American-born Englishman Robert Louis Jefferson attempted to ride entirely unsupported from London to Moscow and back in fewer than fifty days. He endured hard miles on terrible Russian roads, on a meagre diet of black bread, curdled milk, sardines and vodka, arriving home forty-nine days later and two stone lighter.

With the advent of motor vehicles following behind record-breaking riders, some of the adventurous romance of the solo ride was lost. In 1984, Nick Sanders's 79-day, 13,000-mile ride around the northern hemisphere revived the idea of unsupported long-distance record breaking, and Mark Beaumont's record-breaking round-the-world ride in 2008 attracted huge media coverage. Subsequent riders, such as Vin Cox, Alan Bate and Mike Hall, have gone even faster, and spawned a revival in long-distance rides against the clock. Events like the Tour Divide, the Trans-Am Bike Race and the Transcontinental Race have revived the idea of long-distance, unsupported bike racing.

There is, of course, an unavoidable tension between going fast and exploring. The faster you go, the less chance you will have to experience the places you travel through. It's a syndrome that can affect even a non-competitive touring cyclist who is keen to meet a certain daily mileage target. But for most long-distance adventurers, the journey to the limits of mind and body is at least equal in importance to the physical journey on the road; for these riders, riding a bike as far and as fast as possible is a voyage of self-discovery.

FEAR

As he sank the blade of his machete into his shin, even before the pain hit, what gripped the British touring cyclist Ian Hibell was panic. The white heat of pure, blind, heart-stopping panic. There is never a good moment to make a gash in your leg, right down to the bone, and one of the worst places in which to do so is Atrato Swamp in South America, a thirty-mile-wide crust of jungle floating on water hundreds of feet deep, infested with crocodiles, snakes and deadly mosquitoes. Hibell was part of a three-man team cycling across Colombia's Darién Gap, the missing link in the Pan-American Highway, the world's longest road, that runs between Chile and Alaska. The three men spent their days hacking through the dense, thorn-laden vegetation, wading, scrambling and crawling through muddy water, sometimes neck-deep, hauling their bicycles and belongings. At night they slept in hammocks hung from trees clear of the water. Two kilometres was a good day's progress.

As the fetid water of the swamp turned red with blood, Hibell feared this was the end, that he would never catch up with his companions, or worse, that they wouldn't come back to find him. Tensions were running high in the group; the crossing was so much harder than they had anticipated that it was fast becoming a case of each man for himself. Fashioning a rough bandage to stop the bleeding, Hibell crawled on, and did manage to rejoin the pair. After twenty-five days, all three reached the other side of the

swamp. It ranks as the most extreme bicycle journey ever undertaken. So traumatized were Hibell's companions that they abandoned the expedition and joined a local monastery. Hibell continued alone and became the first cyclist to travel the entire length of the American continent.

Whenever I'm out riding and things take a turn for the worse, the thought of Ian Hibell slowly hacking his way through the Atrato Swamp helps me gain a bit of perspective. As bad as things might get, they're very unlikely to get that bad.

It's a rare person who doesn't experience some feelings of trepidation before they set off on a long bicycle journey. We imagine all the bad things that might happen out on the road. We worry about not being mentally or physically up to the challenge. Fear is a healthy emotion when it guides you away from danger, but let it take a grip and you start to see a new horror lying in wait around every corner. Overcoming fear is one of the greatest challenges in setting out on a bicycle adventure. It is also one of its greatest rewards.

QUEST

The writer John Steinbeck knew a thing or two about travel. 'A journey is a person in itself; no two are alike', he wrote, 'and all plans, safeguards, policing, and coercion are fruitless. We find after years of struggle that we do not take a trip; a trip takes us.' The bicycle being a relatively modern invention, and reliant on roads, tracks and paths, cyclists rarely earn the distinction of getting anywhere first. But that hasn't stopped people dreaming up the most fantastically imaginative bicycle quests.

Cousins Nicholas and Richard Crane took the new pursuit of mountain biking to its literal conclusion by pushing, carrying and, very occasionally, riding their machines to the top of Mount Kilimanjaro. They later journeyed 'to the centre of the earth'; having calculated the point on the earth's surface that is furthest from the sea, the pair rode lightweight road bikes for 58 days and 3,300 miles across the plains of India, the mountains of Tibet, and the Gobi, Taklamakan and Dsungarei deserts to reach their 'pole of inaccessibility'.

Cyclists have set off to ride around Britain's 4,000 miles of coastline, followed in the cart tracks of American pioneers on the Oregon Trail, traced the River Danube from its source in the Black Forest to its mouth in the Black Sea and traversed the length of Africa's Great Rift Valley. Cyclists have followed in the footsteps of pilgrims to Santiago de Compostela and retraced Robert Louis Stevenson's walk across the Cévennes and the poet Edward Thomas's 1913 ride from London to Somerset. As if following the route of the 1914 Giro d'Italia wasn't tough enough, travel writer Tim Moore rode it on a period bicycle – single speed with wooden wheels – and then rode a small-wheeled shopper into the Arctic Circle. The young T.E. Lawrence rode a bicycle around France to make a study of Crusader castles, and historian Graham Robb travelled Europe by bicycle to uncover the secrets of Celtic civilization and challenge the assumption that it was the Romans who laid out Europe's first network of straight roads. In 2014, fat biker Daniel Burton rode 775 miles from the edge of the Antarctic continent to the South Pole.

A quest gives a journey a purpose, a ready-made shape and a character, a way of explaining the thing to others and a sense of achievement once completed. It can be a frivolous flight of fancy or a deeply serious project. It can be defined by geography, history, culture or a purely imaginative construct. In December 1967 the artist Richard Long set out from St Martin's School of Art in London and rode north into the countryside. He continued for three days and nights of almost non-stop cycling. Lashed to his bike were sixteen long wooden sticks, and at intervals along his journey he placed each one into the ground, eventually encircling an area of 2,401 square miles. *Cycling Sculpture 1–3 December 1967* is one of Long's earliest – and largest – works of art, not that you will ever find it in a gallery.

Long's sculpture has something in common with what psychogeographers term a *dérive*, or 'drift'. This is a journey deliberately unplanned and directed not by a map, but by the emotions and thoughts triggered by the landscape, architecture and events that the *dériviste* encounters along their way. Perhaps the most satisfying journeys are those that combine elements of the quest and the *dérive*, a framework of planning that is loose enough to allow for plenty of serendipitous detours and diversions.

HUNGER

A good reason for riding a bike with a Brooks saddle is that, if things get really tough, you can always eat it. To do so wouldn't be entirely without precedent. Snowbound in California's Sierra Nevada mountains, the ill-fated wagon-train migrants of the Donner Party resorted to eating their leather clothing and bootlaces, before moving on to eat one another.

There are no known cases of cyclists dying of starvation, resorting to cannibalism, or even eating their leather saddles, yet hunger is a regular companion on any long-distance bicycle journey. Its most acute form is the 'bonk' or the 'hunger knock' that's so familiar to racing cyclists: the empty, wobbly feeling with its attendant cold sweat and grey pallor, the difficulty in thinking straight, and the sheer impossibility of any forward motion. For the touring cyclist, it takes a more latent form: an almost constant need to eat, a heightened concern about where the next meal might be found and a permanent fear that supplies are insufficient.

Pole of Inaccessibility

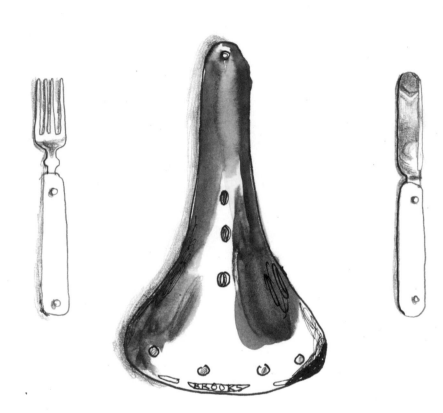

Hunger

Riding a loaded bike every day brings a fierce appetite. A handful of plain ingredients becomes the most delicious of banquets – everything tastes better when it's eaten while lounging beside a fast-running stream under the dappled midday sun, or cooked on a campfire beneath a blanket of stars. Eating is just another aspect of the immersive quality of bicycle travel. Changes in food mirror changes in landscape, climate, culture and history, and nowhere more so than in riding the length or breadth of Europe, where regional and local foods can change within a single day's riding. There is no guest at the table more grateful than the hungry cyclist. Having subsisted on a repetitive diet of packet noodles, dried biscuits and other utilitarian fare, the pleasure of a home-cooked meal – enjoyed as the entire family looks on at the curious foreigner seated at the table – is enough to bring a tear to the eye. Many long-distance cyclists make the heart-warming discovery that the poorer a country and its people, the greater the hospitality they extend to passing travellers.

But food can also be a challenge, and it's a rare touring cyclist who hasn't flinched when presented with some unusual and unappetizing local speciality, be it a bowl of tripe soup (rubber bands, flavoured with beef), a plateful of deep-fried locusts (crunchy, a hint of peanuts) or a whole boiled rat (like a sausage, a furry sausage). Whatever it is, it's unlikely to be worse than eating a leather bicycle saddle.

LOADED

At a time when no bicycle adventure is complete without its own blog or Instagram feed, an essential post is the kit list. The best of these are illustrated with a photograph showing every item carefully arranged in a neat grid. I find these images fascinating. There's something liberating about boiling down the bare necessities of life into what you can carry on a bike. It's also revealing to see the hard choices that the cycling traveller must make, as well as to learn the home comforts that are just too hard to leave behind. (Yikes, only one spare pair of socks! But look! There's not just a miniature espresso maker, but a hand-operated coffee grinder too!)

There was precious little space for luggage on a penny-farthing, so the earliest cycle adventurers had no choice but to travel light. In the 1880s, Thomas Stevens became the first man to ride around the world. He was quite the minimalist. His kit list comprised the following: a single set of clothes and a spare set of underwear; a pistol and ammunition; a length of rope; spare spokes, a rear tyre and a bottle of oil; his writing materials; medicines; and a 'gossamer rubber suit' for when it rained. Crossing Asia he added to this assortment a makeshift 'bicycle tent': a sheet of lightweight cotton boiled in linseed oil, with his bicycle serving as the central pole.

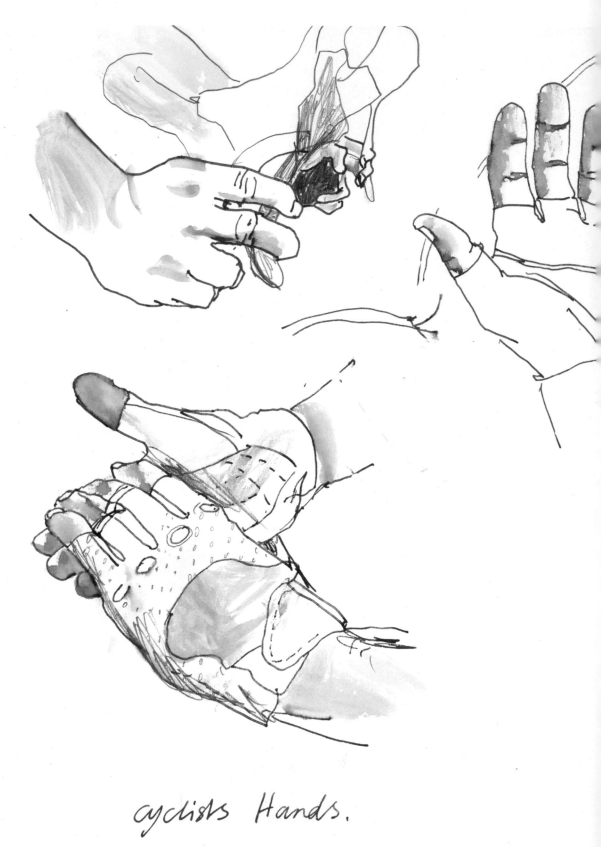

cyclists Hands.

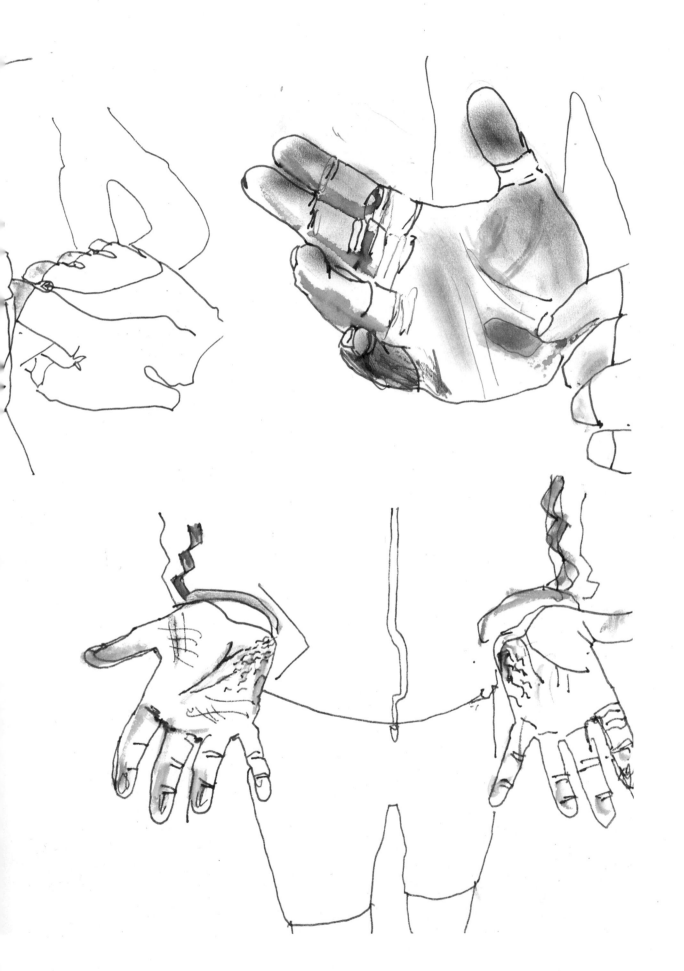

In those days, 'camping' was the reserve of armies on the move, overland migrants and vagabonds. The reinvention of camping as a respectable middle-class leisure pursuit came in the 1890s with the arrival of the 'safety bicycle', which was much better suited as a beast of burden than the high-wheeler. In 1898, Thomas Hiram Holding took what may well have been the first ever cycle-camping holiday, to the west coast of Ireland. Soon after, he founded the Association of Cycle Campers and wrote the first *Camper's Handbook*. Even so, cycle campers were a small minority and most cycle tourists preferred to stay in guesthouses, taverns or the youth hostels that opened up across Europe between the wars.

During the inter-war years, a clear cultural divide emerged on either side of the English Channel: British cycle tourists preferred a bag fixed behind the saddle, while French *cyclotouristes* favoured bags attached to the handlebars above the front wheel.

In 1949, Louise Sutherland set off to ride from London to Land's End with her belongings packed in a trailer she towed behind a bike bought at a jumble sale. This was just the start of her adventure; over the next four decades the diminutive New Zealander rode 40,000 miles through 54 countries and became the first cyclist to ride the length of the Trans-Amazonian Highway. Japanese manufacturers in the late 1960s and 1970s brought lighter, stronger, cheaper bikes with more gears and greater luggage capacity to the market. This made panniers an increasingly popular choice. The 1976 Bikecentennial event saw tens of thousands of Americans touring their country by bike, and an 'everything including the kitchen sink' approach to cycle touring soon became the norm.

At the other end of the spectrum, Richard and Nicholas Crane were obsessed with saving weight on their daring bicycle adventures of the 1980s. They sawed the ends off their gear shifters, spanners and toothbrushes, took the absolute minimum of clothing and slept in lightweight bivvy bags instead of tents. The Cranes foreshadowed the current trend for 'bikepacking', a combination of adventure cycling and ultra-lightweight backpacking in which hard-wearing 'soft luggage' replaces bulky panniers and metal racks. The bikepacker's nylon-frame bag and tightly wrapped handlebar roll is uncannily reminiscent in design, if not materials, of the canvas and leather luggage used by the cycle-adventurers of the 1890s. The wheel has come full circle.

BREAKDOWN

In 2001, at the age of twenty-four, Alastair Humphreys set off to ride around the world. Three years in, having ridden across Europe, the length of Africa and the Americas, he found himself in Siberia, in winter. Everything about riding a bike becomes unimaginably difficult when the temperature drops as low as -40°C, far colder than a home freezer. Flat tyre? Begin by getting out the stove to defrost it, as it's frozen solid to the rim. Be careful not to burn the rubber or let your fingers get stuck to the frozen metal. Replace the tube then inflate the tyre, keeping your fingers crossed that the rubber pump nozzle, whch is frozen brittle, won't shatter. If it does, get out the superglue, stick it back together and carry on. As you're not pedalling, your body temperature is dropping fast, so you'll need to stop regularly to do a 'chicken dance' to keep warm. Though frustrating and time-consuming, punctures were the least of Humphreys' worries. The Siberian roads were a treacherous ice rink and crashes were a daily occurrence; food was scarce and settlements few and far between. But it was exactly the kind of extreme adventure Humphreys had been hoping for, and he looks back on those three months as the most memorable and satisfying of the entire trip.

It doesn't take a ride through the Siberian winter to discover that travelling by bike makes harsh demands of both rider and machine. A hundred times lighter than the smallest car and a fraction of the weight of its rider, a bicycle – even a stout touring machine – is a weightless wonder, a filigree skeleton of metal and rubber, each part slimmed to the minimum while still retaining its essential function. A viable human-powered vehicle must be lightweight – this is part of its genius, but it is also its Achilles' heel. Mechanical failure is a fact of bicycling life, be it a broken spoke on the South Downs Way or a fractured frame on the Karakoram Highway, not to mention any of many mysterious mechanical maladies that demand our attention with their disturbing clunks, squeals, creaks and crunches.

When the professional racing cyclist detects a bit of brake rub, he merely raises a hand: the team car comes alongside and a mechanic leans out of the window to fix it, or, failing that, to furnish him with a new bike. The touring cyclist is alone, hours or even days from help. Spokes break, chains snap, bolts shear, tyres rip, cables fray and bearings seize. Learning how to fix the thing yourself, or if the situation is more grave, finding a backstreet welder who'll do it for you, is part and parcel of making a long-distance journey by bike. However great the promise of new materials and technologies – from Kevlar tyres to carbon-fibre belt drives to internal gearing systems – the unbreakable, maintenance-free bike will forever remain an unreachable dream.

STEED

Of all the oddballs and eccentrics among two-wheeled travellers, there are few to rival Irishwoman Dervla Murphy and Frenchman Bernard Magnoloux. Murphy turned her back on a tough upbringing in socially conservative postwar Ireland to fulfil a childhood dream of riding her bike to India. She fended off bandits, wolves and would-be rapists and rode through deserts and blizzards. Magnoloux quit his job as a teacher to cycle the world in search of love and adventure. He rode for five years and 77,000 kilometres. His innocent, happy-go-lucky demeanour got him into and out of trouble: he was robbed at gunpoint, suffered severe bouts of illness, survived the baking sands of the Sahara and the freezing passes of Tibet, accumulating a never-ending succession of mechanical disasters.

Both cyclists named their bicycles Rosinante, after Don Quixote's horse in Miguel de Cervantes's novel. The name is wordplay by Cervantes, combining *rocín*, the Spanish for an old nag, with the suffix *-ante*, which signifies the animal's metamorphosis in Quixote's imagination. He looks at the worn-out old hack and sees the handsome steed befitting a noble knight-errant. Rosinante is the perfect name both for Murphy's heavy single-speed roadster, with its oil-bath chain case, and Magnoloux's second-hand tourer, encrusted with dust, rust, stickers and bottle caps, upturned handlebars and ragged luggage. Both bikes were undoubtedly old nags, but were the best that their owners could afford at the time. Each bicycle grew into a trusted companion that saw its rider through good times and bad. Rosinante is probably the most popular of all the names touring cyclists give their bicycles.

Some frown at the idea of giving a bicycle a name, attributing it with character traits, or developing feelings of affection for what is, ultimately, just a collection of metal and rubber. Save your love, they chide, for the things that can love you back.

Yet a bicycle is not quite an inanimate object, like a hammer or a table. In his *Ode to Bicycles*, Chilean poet Pablo Neruda sees passing bicycles as whirling, whirring, translucent insects humming through summer. He notes that it is only when bicycles are in motion that they 'have a soul'. When leant against a wall or lying on the ground they are 'cold skeletons'.

A well-ridden bicycle can be a well-loved thing. Mass-produced objects are identical to each other; it is only their imperfections that make them unique. Each chip and blemish tells a story. In his surrealist novel *The Third Policeman*, Flann O'Brien muses on the notion that cyclists may gradually and imperceptibly be exchanging molecules with their machines, merging their identities. The most transcendent moments on a bike occur when we forget we are riding a machine and instead feel as though we're flying through the air, suspended a few inches above the ground. That a machine weighing just a few kilograms can give us such extraordinary sensations is an inexhaustible source of wonder; that we can travel in this manner across entire continents is nothing short of miraculous.

FRAMING THE
MOMENT

Geoff Dyer

RAYMOND DEPARDON

La ferme du Garet (The Garet Farm)
Villefranche-sur-Saône, 1991

I am always struck by the way that riding a bike remains such a childlike pleasure. Even now, in dreary middle age, if I'm cycling through Hyde Park, it takes me right back to the freedoms offered by my first ever racing bike – especially if I'm wearing shorts – bought as a Christmas present after I passed the 11-plus. So the bike is not just a symbol and a reminder of the short-trousered, bare-legged and unselfconscious freedom it promised as a child – it extends that freedom and renews the promise on a daily basis.

HELEN LEVITT

Broken Mirror
New York, 1942

As a child, when you're given a bike, it's not just a vehicle, it's like
a passport to a wider world, as if you can pass to another side
of a mirror – as in Helen Levitt's classic New York pictures from
the 1930s and 1940s. In her pictures she is not just showing
children, but conveying what is going on in a child's head. For
a medium such as photography, which is wedded to the depiction
of the 'external world', this is a remarkable thing to be able to do.

HENRI CARTIER-BRESSON

A bass player on the road Belgrade-Kraljevo,
to play at a village festival near Rudnick

Serbia, 1965

As well as taking you to places, a bike can double as a trolley, as this famous image by Henri Cartier-Bresson reminds us. A bike is a great way of carrying not just human beings, but also their stuff.

ABBAS

Tiergarten

West Berlin, Germany, 1988

(overleaf)

Getting into – or out of – a car is a horrible contortion. As for the parking… With a bike, when you're tired or want to laze in the sun you can just throw it down and go to sleep, whether you're on a country road or in the Tiergarten, Berlin's inner-city park (as in this strange and slightly perplexing image by Abbas).

LIU HEUNG SHING

Tiananmen Square
Beijing, 1989

Healthy, convenient, cool, a bike, in certain conditions, can also
be a way of avoiding the might of the state, as this famous image
by Liu Heung Shing shows. It was taken soon after the storming
of Tiananmen Square in 1989. In addition to this value – and
despite the circumstance in which it was made – the picture also
captures the romance of the bicycle.

BRUNO BARBEY

REUNION. A boy plays in
the Riviere of Galets
Réunion, 1991

The history of photography shows us the many ingenious uses
of the bike. Jacques Henri Lartigue's early work features several
flying machines which are, effectively, flying bikes. This is not
surprising, given that Orville and Wilbur – the Wright brothers
– ran a bike sales and repair shop. What is surprising is that in
this photograph, it seems one might also swim with a bicycle.

ALEX WEBB
Untitled
Munich, Germany, 1991

Being on a bike gives us the chance to see the world as a street
photographer does, but without all the boring waiting around,
the tedium of lugging around equipment and worrying about
exposures, depth of field and so on. The street photographer's
method involves walking – and that's the great disadvantage of
cycling: you can't easily and safely take photographs while you're
riding. But sometimes the cyclist stands in for the figure of the
street photographer, waiting in a state of highly alert patience
for the moments when life arranges itself in those perfectly
symmetrical, sometimes implausibly serendipitous ways that
make for great photographs. Here the bespoke wheel is echoed
by the hole in the bridge that has the surfer in its crosshairs.
In a way it's a projected self-portrait of Webb, the master,
at work.

ROBERT CAPA

Near Nicosia, Sicily, July 28th, 1943
An Italian soldier straggling behind a column
of his captured comrades as they march towards
a Prisoner of War camp.

As the caption makes plain, the picture doesn't tell the whole
story! But that's why Capa framed it as he did – and by so doing
he proposes or suggests an entirely different narrative – a whole
novel, in fact, in a single image. For my money this is just about
the most romantic picture ever taken. It's also a reminder of how,
in photography, as Capa's friend Henri Cartier-Bresson once
said, 'You can reconfigure the world totally just by shifting a few
inches or degrees to the left or right.'

GUY KESTEVEN
As work and entertainment shift ever more into the virtual ether, that visceral connection with the world you get from riding a bike is going to be even more valuable and vital than ever.

ANDREA MENEGHELLI
In the future bicycles will help mankind reconnect with themselves and with nature. Consider the popular saying amongst motorcyclists: 'Four wheels move the body, two wheels move the soul.' Two pedals elevate it, I add. Cycling is cathartic.

LAWRENCE BRADLEY
At the height of my bicycle obsession I was the proud owner of seventeen bicycles. Seriously – seventeen! But I don't need a bicycle museum, what I need in the future is a bike that combines beauty with craftsmanship, reliability and ease of use, and has multiple uses.

FUTURE
CYCLES

Illustrations by
Joe MacLaren

LUKE THOMSON
A child does not care about gizmos
on their first bike; they might love the colour,
or a graphic detail, but more than that they thrill in
the sensation of balancing and riding, the effort that
reaps reward. We as adults need to connect with
that first impression, embrace it and
encourage others to share our passion;
in this way we will nurture the
future of cycling.

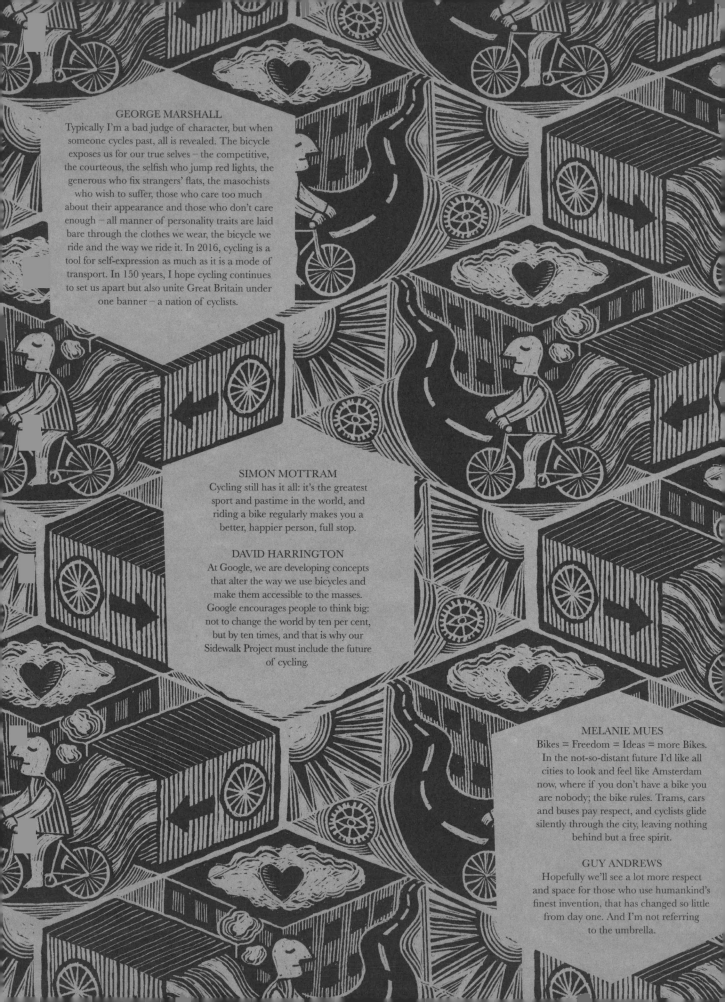

GEORGE MARSHALL
Typically I'm a bad judge of character, but when someone cycles past, all is revealed. The bicycle exposes us for our true selves – the competitive, the courteous, the selfish who jump red lights, the generous who fix strangers' flats, the masochists who wish to suffer, those who care too much about their appearance and those who don't care enough – all manner of personality traits are laid bare through the clothes we wear, the bicycle we ride and the way we ride it. In 2016, cycling is a tool for self-expression as much as it is a mode of transport. In 150 years, I hope cycling continues to set us apart but also unite Great Britain under one banner – a nation of cyclists.

SIMON MOTTRAM
Cycling still has it all: it's the greatest sport and pastime in the world, and riding a bike regularly makes you a better, happier person, full stop.

DAVID HARRINGTON
At Google, we are developing concepts that alter the way we use bicycles and make them accessible to the masses. Google encourages people to think big: not to change the world by ten per cent, but by ten times, and that is why our Sidewalk Project must include the future of cycling.

MELANIE MUES
Bikes = Freedom = Ideas = more Bikes. In the not-so-distant future I'd like all cities to look and feel like Amsterdam now, where if you don't have a bike you are nobody; the bike rules. Trams, cars and buses pay respect, and cyclists glide silently through the city, leaving nothing behind but a free spirit.

GUY ANDREWS
Hopefully we'll see a lot more respect and space for those who use humankind's finest invention, that has changed so little from day one. And I'm not referring to the umbrella.

LAURA QUICK
In 150 years, I imagine bikes will be, in essence, what they are now. They transcend race, class, geographic boundaries and beliefs. They are the absolute opposite of a yacht, for no one could feel alienated upon hearing that you own one.

JOE W. HALL
It's not just physically transportive, it's culturally progressive. Whether you're a schoolkid in the city or a doctor in the countryside, riding a bike is a beautiful and democratic pursuit.

GEOFF DYER
The future for cycling looks brighter – more fun, more glamorous and more popular – than ever, as more and more people realize that car culture is dirty, noisy and doomed.

BARBARA BIGOLIN
Man-bike: a symbiosis for ever and ever. The man learns to balance on the bike, yet the bike asks the man to pedal to provide the balance ... Always on the move!

KIT HOONG TAN
You know, bicycles have always been about getting you from place to place in the most economic and efficient way, and this still holds true, which is quite an achievement when you consider all the vehicles that have come and gone since the bike was first invented. Bicycles are likely to continue evolving and as long as it's the easiest, cheapest and fastest way to get you to where you want to go, there'll be cycling for the next 150 years.

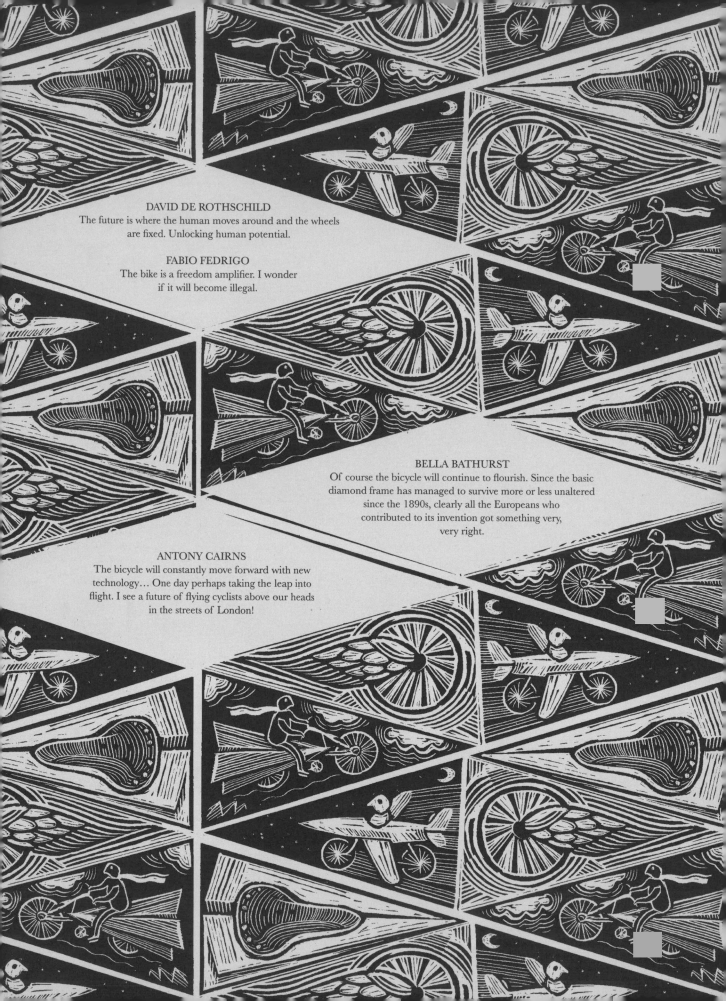

DAVID DE ROTHSCHILD
The future is where the human moves around and the wheels
are fixed. Unlocking human potential.

FABIO FEDRIGO
The bike is a freedom amplifier. I wonder
if it will become illegal.

BELLA BATHURST
Of course the bicycle will continue to flourish. Since the basic
diamond frame has managed to survive more or less unaltered
since the 1890s, clearly all the Europeans who
contributed to its invention got something very,
very right.

ANTONY CAIRNS
The bicycle will constantly move forward with new
technology… One day perhaps taking the leap into
flight. I see a future of flying cyclists above our heads
in the streets of London!

ROB O'BRIEN
Can we ensure the future of bikes is independent
of non-human power? If new, powered components are
essential to the usability of a bike, they should only need solar
or dynamo power, because I don't want my bike to
become yet another thing I have to remember
to charge before I use it.

GASPARE LICATA
Bicycles are the only vehicles you will enjoy all your life:
you start riding when you are two years old and you might still
ride when you are ninety.

PAUL HAWKINS
While there is still space for cycles, there will be cyclists.
When the space becomes less, there will be cyclists. When all
other forms of transport cease, there will still be cyclists.

ACKNOWLEDGMENTS

This book is the result of great team work. Thanks must go to Michela Raoss, Fabio Fedrigo and Andrea Meneghelli, who led the project together with Guy Andrews and Melanie Mues. Among the many people who contributed along the way, with ideas and comments, a special mention goes to James Holland and Oliver Parsons. We also thank Barbara, Lucia and Francesca Bigolin, shareholders of the Selle Royal Group, Nicola Rosin and Antonio Scotto, members of the Selle Royal Group Board, and Cristina Würdig, managing director of Brooks England, who really believed in the project. Brooks's 150th anniversary would not have been possible without the vision of Barbara Bigolin and Massimo Losio. They created, motivated and empowered the passionate people who now work for the future of Brooks. Finally, we are grateful to John Macnaughtan and Adrian Williams of Pashley, who rescued Brooks England when the Raleigh Group faced hard times in 1999. Their love for Brooks led them to pass the responsibility to revive the company to Selle Royal in 2002.

The Brooks Team

SPECIAL THANKS

We truly appreciate the help and support we received from all of the contributors who decided to embrace this ambitious project. As we were near finishing this book we also reached out to the friends of Brooks within the cycling community and asked for their support. Their generosity meant that we were able to produce 150 special edition copies. Therefore, those 150 people who bought the publication in advance deserve not only our gratitude, but also to be mentioned among those who contributed. They are listed here as patrons of the book.

PATRONS OF THE BOOK

Steven William Carr
Bregan Koenigseker
Nicolò Ildos
Ugo Villa
Virgilio Meneghelli
Alfonso Mario Stefanelli
Alex Pataca
Thomas Rosenkranz-Turlon
Dimitrios Tzililis
Joseph Farran
Karin Weis
Lawrence Kelly
Graeme T. Howell
Malcolm J. Greer
Gert Behrmann
Justin Nathaniel Smith
Stuart Bartali Tagg
Rainer Soffke
Jason Michael Holland
Todd Hughes
Richard McCaig
Ken Farran
Jess Jethwa
Russell J. Loome
Mike Waffles McGrath
Aaron Kamp
Toh Ghee Chuan
Egbert Klein Nulent
Adam Leddin
Brian Fung
Lawrence P.H. Bradley
Louis G. Tassinary
David Burles
Alastair Meikle
Paul Hawkins
Kevin Severs
Mark Adams
Nicholas K. Reiter

Carlos Estrella Quintero
Brian Mikiten
Jon Hayt
Klaus Danner
David Browne
Jason Oliver
Eduardo Vidaurreta
Patrick Stevens
Christopher Holt
Paola Rigamonti
Roy T. Zahn
Chris Woudstra
Khwanchanok Suwanchumem
Phil Hargreaves
Marc Vissers
Nicola Rosin
Jaime Alberto Castillo-Leon
Richard Rousseau
Paull Goodall
Ruisjalka Ripakinttu
Mark A. Pace
Ragnar Holm Aasan
Michael and Laurie Hoose
Carlos Rocca
Christian Donaj
Peter Overduin
Jeffrey H. Baker
Gerard Molloy
André Grote
Isabelle Davidson
Greg Roth
Pippykins Swettenham
Jon Hobden
Richard Molloy
Andrew Ruland
Johan Van Extergem
Scott House
Andy Ruland

Adam Baylis-West
Douglas Penney
Christopher M. Caton
Tan Kit Hoong
Cecil Robbins II
Matthew Greenway
John H. Gamble
Cyril Chermin
Fredrik Fredh
John Derry
Armin Linge
Magnus Fornling
Christian Bláha
Leonard M. Karpen Jr
Gordon Sketchley
Nicholas G. Gomez
James K. Owens
Richard Fu
Gommy Michael Lim
James & Mustoe
Pete Hussey
Ricard Rigall-Torrent
Allan Beaty
DT
Jonas Friberg
Hugh Heaney
Christopher Bacon
Mike Daly
Christian Campers
David Minter
Michael Reifenrath
Keith Turner
Oliver Bowden
Levilance J.M. Silva
Mark Oliver
Stephen Murray
Shaunie Shiny Shoes
Pierpaolo Varvazzo

Neil Macmillan
Seamus Kelly
Martin Czernik
Adrian Brooks
Giorgio Nerpiti
Simon Bell
Mike Cooke
Alan Todd
Andrew Michael Stout
Andy Hulme
Justin Schmidt
Colin Wallis
Luke Thomson
Jelle Tienstra
John Reid
Tom Lovell
Stefan Amato
Jenna C. Herlihy
Alex Gough
Wesley Hatakeyama
Dean Tartaglia
Rainer von Lennep
Jun Sasaki
Paul Bodnar
Peter Smith-Round
Brian Lehman
Gary Kornfield
Jonathan Seely
David James Smith
Matthew Trott
Marco Bommarito
Manuel Fernando Herrera Teuzaba
Tim Fricker
Pat Kofahl
Michael Jahn
Max Nightingale

WRITER BIOGRAPHIES

Bella Bathurst is the author of four books including *The Bicycle Book* (2011), published by HarperCollins. She lives in Herefordshire.

Mark Sutton is a cycling business journalist and the editor of trade news and business resource *CyclingIndustry*. He has been writing about the global cycle trade, the politics of cycling transport and grassroots bicycle advocacy for the past decade.

Guy Andrews is the editor and author of several cycling books. He was the founder and long-time editor of *Rouleur* magazine and now writes, edits and publishes books with the imprint *Bluetrain*.

Guy Kesteven started modifying and building bikes at school. His invention obsession began when studying for a history and archaeology degree, while working in a bike shop to pay his way. He's been testing bikes professionally for nineteen years, only a year less than he's been riding his Brooks Swift – but looking at the two, the saddle has definitely aged better.

Joe W. Hall pedals in and around London and, occasionally, the EU. He has written for Rapha's website and also for *Mondial*, *Rouleur*, *frieze*, and *Port* magazines. (He is also an advocate of the Oxford comma.)

Amy Sherlock is a writer, editor and cycling enthusiast based in London. She is deputy editor of art and culture magazine *frieze*.

David Millar was a professional bike racer for over fifteen years. His two books, *Racing Through the Dark* (2012) and *The Racer* (2015), are warts-and-all accounts of his turbulent and colourful career in the world of professional bike racing.

Jack Thurston is a writer and author of *Lost Lanes*, a series of books on the best places to ride in the UK. He also founded and presents *The Bike Show*, the eclectic cycling radio show and podcast established in 2004.

Geoff Dyer is a critically acclaimed author and Fellow of the Royal Society of Literature. His many books include *But Beautiful* (1991), *The Ongoing Moment* (2007) and *White Sands* (2016).

IMAGE CREDITS

First published in the United Kingdom in 2016 by
Thames & Hudson Ltd in association with
Brooks England Ltd

www.thamesandhudson.com

First published in 2016 in hardback in the United
States of America by Thames & Hudson Inc.

www.thamesandhudsonusa.com

A book conceived by
Fabio Fedrigo, Andrea Meneghelli, Michela Raoss
Editor: Guy Andrews
Art director and designer: Melanie Mues,
Mues Design
Picture researcher: Jo Walton

The Brooks Compendium of Cycling Culture © 2016
Brooks England Ltd
Texts © 2016 the authors

British Library Cataloguing-in-Publication Data
A catalogue record for this book is available
from the British Library

Library of Congress Catalog Card Number 2016951960

www.brooksengland.com

ISBN 978-0-500-51960-8

Printed and bound in Italy by
Conti Tipocolor s.p.a.